Wolf Warriors IV
Wolves of Light and Darkness

Edited By
Sherayah Witcher

ISBN 978-1-945247-24-8

WOLF WARRIORS IV: WOLVES OF LIGHT AND DARKNESS

Copyright © 2017 by Jonathan W. Thurston

First Edition, 2017. All rights reserved.

A Thurston Howl Publications Book
Published by Thurston Howl Publications
thurstonhowlpublications.com
Lansing, MI

Cover image by Tabsley

Edited by Sherayah Witcher

Printed in the United States of America
10 9 8 7 6 5 4 3 2 1

TABLE OF CONTENTS

ACKNOWLEDGMENTS

Wolves of Darkness by Chris Albert Copyright © 2017 by Chris Albert

East of the Midnight Sun, West of the Full Moon by Shannon Barnsley Copyright © 2017 by Shannon Barnsley

Prey by Sarah Brigham Copyright © 2017 by Sarah Brigham

Collage by Kersten Christianson Copyright © 2017 by Kersten Christianson

We Have a Lot to Learn by Linda Crate Copyright © 2017 by Linda Crate

The Night dreamer by Anna Crystal Copyright © 2017 by Anna Crystal

Untitled Poem by Timothy Dutton Copyright © 2017 by Timothy Dutton

Keeper of Balance by Christian Esche Copyright © 2017 by Christian Esche

One by Christian Esche Copyright © 2017 by Christian Esche

Cora Dens with Wolves by Kate Falvey Copyright © 2017 by Kate Falvey

A Tale of Two Wolves by Richelle Gardner Copyright © 2017 by Richelle Gardner

Lycanthrope Therapy by Jaime Gonzalez Copyright © 2017 by Jaime Gonzalez

Wolf's Life by Ilona Hegedus Copyright © 2017 by Ilona Hegedus

How Wolves Changed the River by Lana Highfill Copyright © 2017 by Lana Dean Highfill

The Change by Lana Highfill Copyright © 2017 by Lana Dean Highfill

Peaceful Coexistence by Diane Jackman Copyright © 2017 by Diane Jackman

Pain is Relative by Katja Kaine Copyright © 2017 by Katja Kaine

Guardians of Light by Patricia Lehtola Copyright © 2017 by Patricia Lehtola

Ravens Watch at Twilight and Dawn by Patricia Lehtola

To my best friend. You know who you are. Stuck like glue. Always.

Also to Connor, Travis, Kelly, Evelyn, Suzanne, Eric, and others who believed in and supported me. Thank you.

Finally to the dear readers of this book. May light be present in your life and the shadows be few and far between.

INTRODUCTION

Wolves have been revered for centuries. It seems that every culture where wolves are indigenous has their own view of them. For some they are the antagonists in fairy tales and merely hungry for their next meal. Yet for others, they are held in the highest regard as one of the wisest creatures in the animal kingdom. Others view them as mysterious, spiritual beings. No matter how one views the wolf, they are important members of the natural world.

This anthology was born because the Editor in Chief of Thurston Howl Publications, Thurston Howl, saw some of the amazing work being posted to the National Wolfwatcher Coalition's social media pages. He saw the opportunities for these works to have a home and a larger impact and in 2014, the very first Wolf Warriors anthology was published. The anthology turned into a howling success, and it became a yearly tradition. In 2016, we decided to try a theme to shake things up a bit. Our Holiday Wolves edition was something that writers and readers alike enjoy, and this year when approached to be the editor of the anthology, I enthusiastically agreed and we decided to go with another theme. This year's Wolf Warriors IV theme is light and darkness.

Throughout this anthology, we have sought to capture the multifaceted nature of the wolf. This anthology illuminates the features and characteristics of wolves in the bright daylight, shedding light onto the magnificent, agile, and gentle creatures they are. Then it shows you the wolf during its most private and fearful hours and under the cover of night. It shows you the wolf at its most vulnerable and sorrowful moments. This really allows the readers to explore the stark and beautiful contrasts of these lovable animals.

So dear readers, I hope you enjoy reading this anthology as much as we have all enjoyed working on it.

Sherayah Witcher
Associate Editor
Thurston Howl Publications

LETTER FROM THE NATIONAL WOLFWATCHER COALITION

History

Seven years ago a group of friends had a vision - form an organization that speaks solely for the wolf. What emerged was the National Wolfwatcher Coalition.

Our statistics speak for themselves: More than fifteen million hits to our website www.wolfwatcher.org; Over 873,000 likes on Facebook, with posts reaching more than a million advocates; Over 3200 supporters follow us on Twitter and nearly 1500 followers found us on Pinterest. We have extended our reach around the world with friends in many foreign countries including France, England, Germany, Italy, Denmark, China, Mexico, Canada, Ukraine, New Zealand and Australia.

The mission of National Wolfwatcher Coalition is straightforward…to educate and advocate for the long-term recovery and preservation of wolves utilizing best available science. We believe in using peer-reviewed data and encourage comments on wolf-related uses following the principles of democracy.

Recipe for Success

We have no membership dues. We do not sell or share our mailing list. We do not send out solicitations begging for money. We do not mail you merchandise you did not request and we do not inundate your inbox with emails. We have an electronic newsletter that we send out when we have important information to share and if you no longer wish to receive the alerts, it is easy to unsubscribe. We rely on social media and supporters who seek us out for information.

The National Wolfwatcher Coalition is an all volunteer organization. While we do have two independent contractors, one who assist with our website and one who serves as our financial manager, our volunteers do the rest. None of our board members or volunteers receives any compensation. Knowing there are wolves on the landscape, fulfilling their ecological niche is enough reward. Each volunteer works from their home and donates their time, energy and talents to educate and advocate for wolves.

We do not maintain an office which helps to keep our expenses down nor do we maintain a facility with captive wolves.

Volunteers - Our Foundation

A core group of volunteers work every day on behalf of wolves. Our volunteers are scattered across the country but work on issues in every region where there is a current population of wolves. Our goal is to find middle ground and encouraging the use of non-lethal methods to resolve conflicts. Volunteers attend meetings, hearings, workshops and participate by providing testimony on a variety of topics including delisting, hunting and trapping regulations.

We are always looking for more volunteers. It doesn't

matter if you have an hour or ten to donate, we can find a job for you! Contact us at info@wolfwatcher.org

We are able to advocate for wolves because of the generous donations from our supporters and through the purchase of shirts and other merchandise available for sale at our website store. The National Wolfwatcher Coalition is also listed as a non-profit organization that you can support with your purchases through smile.amazon.com or through a link on Pinterest. This financial support has allowed us to foster relationships with other like-minded organizations.

We wish to thank Jonathan Thurston for putting together this anthology and donating the proceeds to the National Wolfwatcher Coalition.

These are critical times for wolves. The century old fears, myths and hatred towards the wolf still exist today. Wolves are now a hunted game animal in every state where they have lost their federal protection. Wolf policies allow for liberal killing of wolves involved with conflicts. With today's anti-wolf political climate, it can sometimes be discouraging, but we are a strong pack.

We will not give up the fight for wolves, not today, not tomorrow or the next day. And, with your continuing support, we can insure future generations will hear wolves howl.

Board of Directors
National Wolfwatcher Coalition

WOLVES OF DARKNESS
CHRIS ALBERT

Chris Albert seeks to advocate for wolves and predators, and indeed all wildlife and wild places by observing, educating herself and others, offering health care where possible to wild things (she is a veterinarian), and occasionally creating - perhaps the greatest of human capabilities - the story.

Father wolf stretched out on the hilltop, overlooking his land and watched the sun go out of sight below the horizon. He heaved a sigh of relaxation. It was more than his knowledge of a lifetime; it was a cultural memory: when the last sun of the year sets, the humans are gone, and the world is a much safer place for wolves.

The world would exist in shades of dark, and be the province of the musk ox, the arctic hare, and the wolf in a dance of the ages. People that came this far north to watch often described the dance as a battle with sides and winners and losers: a point of view that would have baffled the animals.

Father wolf howled. The slow, changing, melancholy notes spread over the hills and valleys like a fog, calling his family together. His mate and three youngsters had survived the light times. They were reasonably well fed, and the cold and the dark would be a bit easier for them.

Without any significant sunlight for four months the lichens and other plants of this place would not grow. The plants that were here now were all there would be, and there were not enough for every rabbit and musk ox to survive the long winter.

Without the wolves, they would all starve. With the wolves removing the slightly weakened before they took too much plant material, enough would survive until light-time.

The wolves gathered and moved. They moved by brilliant starlight, and tonight the moon was halfway through its strange arctic cycle: waxing to full and then waning for two weeks. It was not even a hunt, as we would recognize such. It was just movement: a driving curiosity to see what was out there, to cue in on the vulnerabilities of the other inhabitants of the tundra. It could turn into a hunt in a flash, but for now, it was just the movement of seeking.

Wolf puppies are born with the senses to discriminate all the variations of their world, but they don't know what the scents and sounds mean. Probably some of the more obvious ones – like blood – would cause excitement and elicit feeding whether or not there were parents around to model that, but the meaning of more subtle ones – like the smell of a particular bacteria in the hundreds that make up the rumen population of a musk ox, need to be taught.

The pack quickly detected the presence of one of the herds of musk oxen from the methane cloud that emitted from them, like a walking, slow cooking stew. The darkness meant they could not rely primarily on sight to inform them. The parents carefully sniffed the air; the young ones watched, comically cocking their heads. These were the smells that had no meaning – yet – for them. But the parents detected the smell of wounds on two young bulls. They half-heartedly lunged at each animal, but the young oxen were still strong. The youngsters learned: that smell is meaningful, meaningful enough to test the animal, and *that* response means it is too strong to hunt. Musk oxen are as big as cars, and taller – the wolves would be foolish to take on a healthy one. The pack moved on, for now. They would be back. There would be no food tonight.

Does the arctic hare bolt or stay hidden when the pack of wolves comes suddenly upon it? Four bolted, and were immediately snatched by the wolf family. Even the youngsters had learned this skill. With a little food in their belly, they settled down for a nap in the waxing moon.

Clouds rolled in and blotted out the moon and stars. Without some light, even the wolves couldn't take down prey, so they napped some more. Without the daily warming of the sun, the weather was not so volatile, but the big global wind currents still exerted their influence.

Other global influences also came to the lonely high arctic. The spring influx of birds brought "souvenirs" with them from every port of call. Some of the viruses and bacteria were quickly extinguished, and some found a dangerous foothold. This year a deadly disease of ruminants had infected one of the herds of musk oxen. The wolves came upon them.

The small herd, weakened by the virus that had grown in them all summer, were facing the long night already at a disadvantage. Too slow to form their usual protective circle, the wolves killed them all, in a bloody carnage that outrages their detractors.

But like all the deaths of the prey, the loss of one herd was a blessing for the others: The virus stopped there. Digested by the wolves, dispersed by the wind, it did not survive to infect the other herds. Fortunately for our wolf family, the virus did not infect them. This time.

The wolves stayed at the scene of the slaughter until the moon dipped below the horizon for the two week part of its arctic journey. Given time, all such "surplus kills" are devoured. They got the urge to travel before the meat and bones were all gone, but they would remember this "cache" in their "deep freeze" if hard times came.

Setting out in "moondark", but with bright stars, they visited to distant parts of their territory. They were a little anxious as they detected a neighboring wolf pack. Then they were on high alert as they came upon a lone wolf dispersing.

Dispersal is a time of maximum danger for wolves. Alone, only somewhat experienced in the hunt, and without the backup of the family in case of injury, many perish. Who knows whether a neighboring pack will kill the intruder, or cautiously allow it to join. But the reluctance of wolves to mate with family ensures there will always be young ones dispersing and taking their chances, and there will often be packs who accept them.

This young male fared well. The pack, distracted by the plume of scent from another musk oxenherd many miles away, and full bellied from their kill of the virus-infected herd, tolerated his presence on the outskirts of their family. He slowly dared to come closer.

The moon rose again – a month into the dark time. The wolves had slept and travelled, fortified by the occasional arctic hare. But they were hungry. They had been following the plume of the herd for two weeks, and they were coming close.

The parents were excited by one particular smell: as a young cow had matured, the metabolic disease she was born with had become a problem. Her smell was different – sweet. The herd circled when the wolves approached. They patiently retreated. The musk oxen couldn't stay in formation forever; they needed to graze and rest.

As the moon waxed to full, the wolves kept up the pressure: darting in and retreating, then resting. After several days they were becoming desperate; any arctic hares in the area were gone. They were hungry. They were beginning to starve. Still the herd held them off. The musk oxen were grumpy too, their grazing constantly interrupted.

A week into the standoff, one of the pups rushed in, and the herd scattered. They tried to reform, and in doing so the wolf was badly trampled, but the sick cow was also isolated and quickly brought down. The young wolf died; the pack feasted. The death of the young wolf would ease the pressure on the pack to find food. The death of the cow would have happened eventually anyway, and it meant extra food for her herd mate that she might produce a calf this spring.

The pack rested and feasted for several days, then moved on, travelling into a setting moon again. The new male was fully integrated into the pack.

By the next moonrise and moonset, the wolf pack was back in the area of the first herd of the dark time. The wounds had healed on one bull but festered on the other. Millennia of judgment calls, and cultural tradition had honed the instincts of the adult wolves. It was worth the risk to try. The pack was hungry again.

The musk oxen made their defensive circle, but they were now two months into the dark time, and their desperation to eat was high. They did not defend their wounded herd mate very fiercely. He was taken down without injury to the pack. Again, the food he would have eaten was available for the healthy of the herd. Without the wolves, the whole herd would be hungrier and weaker.

By full moon, they had come to the place of the whole herd slaughter. Here, there was still food to be had. It was not warm, and frozen flesh required much time and energy to chew up, but it was food. The pack had done well.

Breeding season approached, and the mother and father mated. The new young male would bide his time. He was part of a family, and unrelated. In time he would sire his own pups, but simply being part of the family was good.

As the light time came closer, life was a bit easier for the wolves. The hares and musk oxen were at the hardest time of their year, and the wolves were thriving. That was this year. In other years, some wolves starved.

Then one day, the light peeked over the horizon. Calves would be born, a new litter of wolf pups would be born, and another layer of anxiety would shadow the wolves as humans invaded their world.

East of the Midnight Sun, West of the Full Moon
Shannon Barnsley

Shannon Barnsley is a writer, poet, and folklore devotee from New Hampshire, currently living in Brooklyn. Growing up playing in thick Northern forests and devouring folklore from as far West as Alaska and as far East as Russia, she has always felt pulled to the feared and mythic Other beyond the fire, be they wolves or more human scapegoats. This led her to a degree in Creative Writing/Mythology & Religion from Hampshire College. Since graduating, she has worked for an independent publishing company, given tours at an 18th century Shaker village museum, and tackled the never-ending quest that is life with multiple chronic illnesses. Her first book, Beneath Blair Mountain, *was published by 1888.*

PART I - WOLF AT THE DOOR

We have always been in the shadows, no matter where we go. Travelers in the night. Exiles. Refugees. Cast out by strangers who had become neighbors and neighbors who had become strangers, until we were nothing but monsters. A tale told to frighten children on long nights. A shiver in the trees. A shadow on the moon. A hush on their grandmother's lips of things they once did to people who once were here.

So my grandmother's own words said. On my mother's side we were foreign twice over, so the story went. Once coming West, once coming East. On my grandfather's side we were from Russia once, before coming East to find a better life in so-called uncharted territory.

Many times I've imagined it, the journey my great-great-so-on-and-so-forth-grandfather must have taken when he set out for Alaska. A lone Ruska Roma werewolf among the Russians and the Inuit, his children marrying into both. We may have disappeared entirely, just another name lost to time and gadje descendants, were it not for the one reminder we can never shake: memories stitched into our skin with every hair on our wolf hide.

So imagine my grandfather's surprise when he found my grandmother. She had been born in Romania, her family coming West with her and her siblings in tow. They were trying to find any life, as far away from the fires and madness consuming Europe as they could go. Somewhere they could disappear and never be found. A safe place, somewhere free, where no one knew them or the secrets they whispered to the moon.

And it was there two long-lost Roma lines were intertwined. Two wolves hearing a strangely familiar call on a dark night in some long ago Alaskan winter. My grandfather, an American born and raised in Alaska, and my grandmother, a refugee and a newcomer to this once-Russian land, fleeing an evil with many names. Porrajmos. Kali Traš. Holokosto. A dark chapter of a long history etched into our DNA. Another story for survivors to tell in hushed tones.

The stories come from both sides of my mother's family, but as my grandfather died before I was born, my grandmother told them all. They bleed together, two sides of the same coin. We lived in sleepy villages until the nightmares grew too many. Then we fled. We found new homes and fled those too. Always on the move, always the strangers welcomed in the night with watchful eyes, always the first to go.

My grandmother told me memories. Hers? Her mother's? My grandmother's grandmother's? My grandfather's grandfather's grandfather's? All of them? The same old story again and again all spun together because it never stops. A wheel that never ceases turning, carrying people who never stop moving.

She had many stories, but in the end they were always the same and she told them like they happened yesterday or are happening now. A new village we passed through, a home we lost when they came. Men who walk among the living with cold hearts and no souls, who spill the blood of others and feed on what's left. And the frightened peasants they whip into frenzied mobs.

They come on horses, uniforms smart as can be. They come on foot with no uniforms. They hunt us, and sometimes they catch us. They take us, and sometimes they kill us. They hate us, and sometimes they hurt us, or they love us, and sometimes they marry us. We live among them, and sometimes we are them. Until we're not.

So people turn the Roma away like a wolf at the door, or hunt them down like animals. But in their quest to be rid of the Gypsies, they let a darker force stoke fires that consume men and nations. They let the vampire in. Let him bleed them dry for the privilege of blaming us.

The dates shift. The faces and the uniforms change. The words we call ourselves and the words they call us come and go, but not much changes. They come, and we go.

Sometimes we were the same, she used to say. Times when there were no words for Us and Them, or the words were interchangeable or all switched up. Sometimes they were like us, and sometimes we were like them, and sometimes no one could tell the difference.

But times change. Borders and allegiances change. Our skin was ripped away, our bones broken, our bodies changed. And their hearts grew cold again, our own staked in the graves where memories and kin were buried. They were our monsters, and we were theirs. Gadjo and Gypsy. Countryman and foreigner. Vampire and werewolf.

Those of us who survived fled. We kept fleeing. We fled and scattered and spread until we somehow wound up in the Land of the Midnight Sun. In a sleepy village where the names are still Russian, even though a new flag has flapped in the wind well over a century. A little place tucked away off the edge of the map where you can't run any farther. As

North as even the North Wind knows. East of the sun and West of the moon.

A place where the sun never seems to stop shining until one day it does, and it isn't seen again. Just like one day the little village wasn't Russian anymore. English trickled in and new faces came. Names changed. Time passed.

New languages came, old languages were forgotten. Children were born, elders were buried. My grandfather met my grandmother. My grandfather died. My mother met my father. My mother left. The snow piles up and buries our memories.

But the past is a hard thing to rub out. Wounds go deep and furrows freeze hard in a land like this. The moon still remembers, and the sun still knows. Old words on old lips, old prayers for old faiths. Old stories. Old secrets. Old sins.

My grandmother is still here, though now the cold in her bones only bothers the birds that pick them clean. My father is still here too. His people have always been here. 12,000 years they've been here. The Russians came and the Americans came and my father's people are still here.

Sometimes they hunted seals for the Russians and sometimes they caught fish for the Americans. Sometimes they are taken and sometimes they are killed. Sometimes they are hated, and sometimes they are hurt, or sometimes they are loved, and sometimes they are married.

They spoke Russian sometimes and English other times. New immigrants came with new tongues to tell their own old stories and even today keep coming, with histories as far-flung as my own. But my father's people are still here.

And now I'm here. With cold Alaskan air blown all the way from Russia in my lungs and that feeling there's a storm coming in my cold Roma bones. Romani. Romany. Gypsies. Iñupiat. Inyupik. Eskimos. Volkodlak. Vârcolac. Werewolf. Our names change, but I'm the same.

Sometimes I am Senka Tarkik, named for a family friend who never made it out of Europe, named for my father. One of two names my father has, one English, one not. So sometimes I am Senka Samson, named for someone I do not know. Someone who helped us? Someone who hurt us? I don't know.

That story wasn't my grandmother's to tell. My father either didn't know it or didn't want me to. Either way I am me. Blood of my mother, blood of my father, blood of the wolf.

My roots come from many places, but one of them is here, so here I stand. In a little building North of the Arctic Circle and 300 miles from the nearest person. Where even the wind shifts nervously, as though unsettled by how North he is or how dark it gets. He whispers.

I hear him as he whispers to the foxes, to the frozen water, to the hardened earth. I whisper back with different tongues on different days, sometimes literally. A woman alone sometimes and sometimes a lone wolf.

A werewolf at the top of the world. I know, it sounds like a story a grandmother would tell to frighten children. That such a thing could be in this day and age. But there are places like here and people like me even now, if you look hard enough. If you listen to the wind whisper secrets through the cracks of old homes and the hollows of old cemeteries, or you find yourself out on dark nights, in witching hours, when your candle flickers in the gust.

The shadows are there. The wind whispers, and they dance. The candle burns brighter, and they flee across the walls.

We think the flame protects us, but it's the flame that casts the shadow. There is no shadow without it. There are no monsters without mobs to drive them out. But the shadow is longer than the flame. The mob forgets at daybreak, when all seems safe again, but the monster remembers.

Our memories run deep as our graves, and we will not forget either. And they both weigh upon me, even at the ends of the earth. Six months I have been working a remote outpost at the very top of nowhere. My father asks when I will come home. My mother and half-sister ask when I will visit them in the Lower 48, or at least take a job somewhere closer to an actual airport. But I am here, and I will stay here. Until I won't.

I like it here. I like the solitude. How the only names I'm called are the ones I choose and the only words I hear are the ones I feel like using. But on those long nights when I feel how very alone and how very North and how very small I am, I grow nervous. I have a radio, but a little thing like the wind can silence it. There is no one here but me, yet some nights a little thing like a shadow can trick me. For shadows are no small thing here.

PART II - PAST THE THRESHOLD

The wind whispers and my neck needles as I set down the lantern. A flame flickers. I look like something out of some time long gone, I'm sure. A witch at the edge of the village. A thief in the night. A stranger on the road. But a lantern does the trick when I don't have my flashlight or my hat with the light on it.

Shadows sweep across the room as I rummage for the can opener. I could flick on the lights. But power is precious here, and I've precious little to spare.

The can burns cold to the touch. A fading label says it's alphabet soup. Letters in a language and an alphabet we didn't always have tumble out at the prompting of a blade. It lands in the tarnished pot with an ungraceful plop.

Gas clicks on and blue flame joins the red one already casting shadows around me. Last night I sank my teeth into warm flesh, the blood hot as it hit my tongue and the virgin snow. Tonight, I burn my tongue on canned soup. I am many things, but hungry is often one of them, and food is food.

I eat my dinner on a little folding table by the light of the lantern. I sing an old folk song from a land I've never known. I play an old hit song from a place I've never been. I radio the only pilot who can reach me out here and arrange the next delivery of supplies. I lay out cards for solitaire like my mother did. I lay out cards for poker like my father did. I lay out cards that are not for solitaire or poker like my grandmother did.

Eventually, I go to bed. I lie awake listening to the foxes, and the wind, and the snow that is either falling to the earth or swirling back up into the air. I think of a boy back home named Ujarak. I think of a girl back home named Skye.

It's a deep shade of midnight outside, so I think I should sleep. But this time of year that's all there is. For two turns of the moon every year the sun hides its face. Polar night falls, and there is only darkness. Not even a dusky hint of dawn.

The moon is all there is until the sun seems to fade from my thoughts. Just a story from some other place, not a part of where I am now and how I live today. The heat hisses and the freezer hums. The foxes yip somewhere. The lullaby lulls me to sleep.

I wake, unsure how long I slept. All night? An hour? Sixteen hours? Only the clock can tell me and if it weren't for military time, I still wouldn't know.

I judge whether I should go back to sleep. Whether I can. Am I tired? Will it help my sleep schedule? Do I even have a sleep schedule? What would be the point of one now?

I check the calendar, remind myself when the shipment comes, how much food I have, how much fuel. I'm losing time. Days run together, and I can't tell them apart in my memories without daylight to separate them.

I boot up the computer, the familiar hums and whirs and start-up noises as it slowly wakes up. Like the 90s never ended and everything since was a dream. Something that happened to someone else, somewhere else. I try to check my e-mail and pray the weather is favorable. The screen flickers a sinister threat of seizures as I wait. I'm good at waiting. I do a lot of it here.

My small victory is dashed when I see the subject lines awaiting me. My mother's growing anxiety is palpable. Even in Seattle she sees things changing. They scare her.

She doesn't know who to trust anymore since her neighbors, the Haddads, got that note telling them to get out and the next week found their screen door torn up. They replaced it with a storm door and found it shattered four days later. The white lady in the house down the road had her tires slashed and an ethnic slur about her three-year-old son spray-painted on the car. My mother doesn't say, but I can tell she's leaving the house less and less.

A rare e-mail from her Romnichal ex-husband, Mike, confirms this. He's worried about her. He asks me to contact her when I can. Maybe I could visit next summer? He wants to do more for her, but it's hard since he moved away. He wants to come see her and my half-sister, but he's busy. His co-worker, Armando, has disappeared, so he has to do twice the work.

My mother always told my grandmother to stop clinging to the fears of the past. This is America, she'd say. This is the 21st century. We're safe now. Those times are over. People know better now.

She doesn't say that anymore.

Maybe it's better I don't visit, she says in another e-mail. Maybe I'm better off where I am, so far from it all, so distant. I feel a weight in the pit of my stomach.

My cousin, Yuka, has written me too. She's doing well at

Iḷisaġvik College. Her friend just got her chin tattooed. She wants to do the same. Maybe then they'll stop asking if she's Asian when she goes to the Lower 48.

My half-sister, Daniela, has sent a link to another article about a protest in Portland. She has a way of getting in all the photos for this kind of thing. This one has a link to some online gallery with more pictures. It takes forever for the damn thing to load, but I have the time. I click through, taking in all the signs. All the anger. All the fear.

I stop at a face so like mine but not quite. One that blends into a crowd better and yet insists on standing out. Daniela has her own tattoos. Hers are from a tattoo artist named Kyle, not someone reviving a dying art, but they claim an identity just the same. I envy Daniela and Yuka both.

In the picture, Daniela's face is striking; concern knit into her brow but resolve set in her jaw. I click through a few more before I see her again. In this one Daniela and one of her housemates, Rachel, are arm in arm. They bear aloft signs that both say "We've seen this shit before". Daniela's also reads "Roma immigration ban - 1885" and Rachel's reads "Jewish refugees turned away at the border - 1939". I click through a few more and see a crowd shot. A white girl in the periphery wears a t-shirt that says "Gypsy Soul".

Somehow I doubt her ancestors died in concentration camps, were driven out of Spain by the Inquisition, or were forcibly sterilized in Czechoslovakia. Everybody wants to play dress-up as a Gypsy, but no one knows how many died. They'll step into our skin and wear us as an accessory, but how many stood by, accessories to mass murder?

At least she showed up, I tell myself. She did something. She cared more than most.

"More than most is a low bar," I whisper to no one.

I feel restless. I want to go outside. It's not so cold today (tonight?). This time of year it's easily 20 below, but it can get as much as 60 below with windchill factors creeping into the 70s. This winter has been mild by my standards. Just yesterday (Or was it more than that? Two days? Three maybe?), it was a downright balmy 39. But it's getting colder again. A stormfront is moving in and the temperature is dropping fast.

I begin donning the many layers it takes to venture out. An odd mesh of synthetic fibers and furs. No vegan will ever convince us Alaskans to give up fur completely. They can argue morality with me when the temperature is as far from freezing as freezing is from a heat wave that makes birds fall from the sky in India. Okay, maybe it's not that cold right now, but the point stands. Polar vortex or polar night or both, suffice to say it gets cold.

I pull a wolf pelt hood down around my ski-masked face and open the door. I brace for the wind, but it still hits me with a sudden sharpness that sucks the breath from the lungs and the warmth from the bones. I step past the threshold.

The world is dark beyond. A new moon and no sun to hold out for. But I know this land. This great, flat expanse of tundra and ways to die. My home. I love it the way a sailor loves the sea. Maybe I'll die here one day. What a thing, to die in the land you lived all your days. A privilege denied to many.

I walk to the nearby structure where the fuel is kept. I measure what's left. Pray it lasts as long as it needs to. I make sure everything else is in order. Coo over my snowmachine like it's a prize-winning Thoroughbred. Back outside, the air is bracing once again. I swear it's even colder.

A streak of movement catches my eye in the black shroud of sky above. Too big and far off to be a bird. A plane maybe? If so, they're going down fast. Very fast. Like a bird in sweltering heat.

Near the river, I think. I could take wolfshape and run to them, but chances are they'll hit the ground and die on impact or freeze to death in the river before I reach them.

And if the snow starts while I'm out there I could get lost in whiteout conditions and never find my way back. They're too far for me to do anything but watch.

I feel that way a lot these days.

I say a prayer in my grandmother's tongue and trudge back inside. A sound makes me jump. The radio!

I fly to it. A mayday crackles through, then silence. I clutch it even so, trying to reach people I know are gone. Like my great-grandmother, who, for years after coming to America, wrote in vain to every agency and surviving friend or relative she could think of, trying to find her sister. She always hoped she never found any news of her because she was a refugee somewhere, her name changed or her whereabouts unknown. My great-grandmother died hoping.

A crackle. Someone else's voice.

"H-hello?" I ask.

"Senka?" says a voice I know. The wife of Norton McGill, the pilot who delivers my supplies. She must have heard me trying to reach the downed plane. "Senka, what is it? Are you okay?"

"Aguta?" My voice sounds strange. "Aguta, I saw a plane go down. There was a mayday. I heard it."

I tell her all I know. She says she'll pass it on to the authorities. In case anyone is looking for the wreckage or remains.

"Senka," she says. "I wasn't going to bother you, but- I'm worried."

"What's wrong?" I ask.

"Osha and Lusa are missing," she says.

"Could they be on a hunt?"

"They left all their gear. They left the dogs." The words crackle. "They're just... gone."

There aren't a lot of us this far North and this far from Barrow. We look after each other. This is an easy place to disappear.

"Amihan thinks they were taken. So does Old Man Norman."

"Taken where? By what?" My voice echoes through the poor connection. More likely they got injured or got lost and froze to death. Or had a run-in with a bear.

"Norton's away," Aguta says. "I'm alone. I'm scared, Senka."

"It's probably nothing." The flames flicker and the shadows grow. "Just bar the door and have your gun by the bed. In case the bears are extra bold."

"Senka..." Something is lost in the interference between us. "...worry about you out there. A woman alone-"

"The safest place for a woman *is* alone," I tell her.

"Just be safe, okay?"

I promise her I will. She still seems unsettled, but we both go. I try to forget her unease. But every flicker of light, every motion out of the corner of my eye sets my nerves on edge. I am alone here, I tell myself.

Completely alone.

I always sleep with a gun out here anyway, but tonight it isn't bears my imagination runs with. I fall asleep thinking of Osha and Lusa. Their broad faces alight with smiles the last time I saw them, on my way up here. In my dreams their smiles falter. Something stalks them.

They scream, and the dream changes. Daniela is screaming now. A man at a protest is stabbing her. Rachel hits him with her sign, but he goes after her next. They lie dead on the pavement, a pile of bodies.

Now it's a mass grave somewhere. They all have symbols on their arms. Some I recognize, some I don't. A lot of them are red triangles. A good number pink. Daniela has a black triangle, like my grandmother might have had they stayed.

Mike's mangled arm bears a brown one. Armando's is blue. Rachel a yellow star.

The men attacking the protestors become men in uniform. They try to bury them, hiding the crimes they boast aren't crimes. A girl in a ripped and bloodied Gypsy Soul t-shirt lies among the bodies, her blonde hair and now wide-open blue eyes not enough to save her after all. Through her torn shirt I make out a port in her chest. On her arm is a black triangle with a yellow one over it.

I try to run away. My breath hangs in the frozen air of some forest in winter. The men are far away, but I feel afraid. I try to run. A Roma woman straight out of an old photograph reaches out to me. I hesitate. A deafening sound booms as the Einsatzgruppen shoot her on sight. She screams and turns into my grandmother and then my mother.

I run, on four paws now. I smell gunpowder and gas. I smell fear. Shelling somewhere. The faraway thunderclap of war, closer every day. My paws hit the petrified earth and powdered snow like ash. I stop short at a sudden drop.

I look down and see the river. A plane goes down, but this one is an old-timey plane. The kind in World War II documentaries. The ones I watched at 2 a.m. when nothing else was on and I was staying with my mother in Seattle.

"Help us!" the pilot begs, but he's too far away and there's nothing I can do. A sudden current carries him away before he knows what's happening. I look up and the sky is black again, cold Russian air like the kind that snakes over the Arctic hits me.

I'm home, but it's different now. I see figures on the tundra. People I know. But none of them look the same.

I look down again, and the river is gone. A village is below me, full of people. But these aren't Romani corpses or Portland protesters. They're Iñupiat, dressed as if they were in a black and white photo from some history book. They turn into Yuka and my father and the rest of my family on his side.

They cry out in Iñupiaq, but I don't know what to do. Then the river rises back up, and they vanish, their voices suddenly silent. I turn and the thing pursuing us is upon me, but I can't see its face. It keeps changing.

I wake up screaming. My clothes are soaked through with sweat even in the cold of Alaskan winter. I reach for the gun, but I know the safety it offers is an illusion. Against bears and the wilderness it's essential. But that's not what I'm afraid of now.

I reach for the Nalgene I sleep with so it won't freeze. Probably unnecessary, but the temperature is still dropping. I gulp down water, spilling some on my chin and shirt. I feel shaky, like someone recovering from a long illness. Or trying to.

I lie alone in the darkness, afraid. Finally, I muster the courage to get my headlamp and make my way to the kitchen. I find my lantern and light it. The shadows change. I sing an old folk song my grandmother used to sing to me, my voice cracking like Aguta's on the radio. I fill the kettle and click the blue flames back into life. I wait, singing another song to myself.

I jump at the sound of the kettle whistling. I feel like a fool. I pour the water into a mug with some evaporated milk and Ovaltine. What I really want is a hot toddy, but this will do. I take a sip and my insides feel warm. I let out a sigh and feel my muscles release. I didn't know quite how tense they were until I feel the weight lifted.

For a while all I do is breathe. I warm my hands on the mug, sipping slowly. I try to clear my mind, but my brain itches to fill the silence.

I worry about Daniela. I know my mother does. She doesn't want her getting involved. Daniela "looks American", she'd be safe, my mother insists. She's fair like Mike.

But someone has to get involved, I tell her every time. If there had been more Danielas, maybe my grandmother would have grown up in Romania. Maybe Rachel's family would never have left Poland. Maybe Armando would be at work with Mike.

News is slow out here, but I know things are changing. People are scared, seemingly on every side. Their nerves are frayed, their energy drained as though by some kind of psychic vampirism. They buy guns and baseball bats or cling to crosses and pretend that will protect them. They bar the door, but the vampire is already inside.

I set down my mug, the dregs forming shapes I think might look like something. A dog perhaps. Or a bear. Outside my little world, the wind shifts. The storm grows closer.

A knock at the door and I nearly leap out of my skin.

My heart and mind race. A knock? How? I'm 300 miles from my closest neighbor. I'm alone out here. Completely alone.

My head snaps to the door as adrenaline floods my system. I turn on the lights and then immediately panic. I felt safer in the dark, where I can blend in, where I'm invisible. Now they know I'm here.

Shouldn't they? If they were here to steal my fuel or murder me, why would they knock? My legs leaden, I walk the arctic entryway. A gust of cold undoes whatever warmth the Ovaltine offered. There, on the threshold stand two men and a dog, framed by the otherworldly glow of the Northern Lights. Ribbons of color snaking through the darkness, a dance as old as there are winters to count.

The dog immediately bolts past me, as if to escape a predator. As if she already knew I was pack.

"Our plane-" says the one man. He has a subtle accent I can't quite put my finger on.

"Just get in!" I order, all but yanking them both inside.
I slam the door shut behind us.

"Thank you!" the other says, taking my hand like a beggar woman about to bless me. He's clearly American. His breath still hangs in the air. "Thank you."

"We barely made it here," says the other man again. "My friend here got banged up in the crash and we're cold. So cold..."

"Well, you're here now," I say. "Come on."

I usher them into the building proper, past the entryway. My little folding table has one chair. The first man takes it, my mug still warm where I abandoned it. The American is happy enough just to collapse onto the floor. The dog nuzzles into him.

Outside, the wind picks up. My neck prickles.

PART III - THE STRANGER

In the light, I get a better look at the men, now freed of their outermost layers. The one on the floor is clearly a pilot, he even has the brown coat and brown fur-lined hat, like a hero out of a war movie. He has a kind face, and I watch him relax as the dog curls up to warm them both.

His eyes are brown, his hair a medium brown as well. He's tall and leggy, like a tree that grew too quickly. He has a hint of stubble, like he's contemplating a beard or could just have been distracted and forgotten to shave.

He's pale from the winter, it's hard not to be, but he's downright tan next to the other man. The one at the table looks as though he was cut from alabaster. His milk white skin is veined through with blue threads. Like an expensive cheese. Or marble.

His features are straight off a statue. Strong jaw, straight nose, clean-cut. Posture like he should be posing on a horse, a sword aloft. His hair is alpine blonde, his eyes a distant kind of grey. His shoulders are broad, the rest of him trim, as though he were cut specifically to look good in a suit and not the other way around.

He looks Nordic, but his accent is something I can't quite place. Just vague enough to seem sophisticated, not enough to misunderstand what he says. He seems guarded, aloof perhaps, less a part of this space than the pilot who's already made himself at home.

Faced with two gentlemen callers, I realize what a mess I must be. My hair unkempt, my clothes sweat-stained, my face windburned. I wasn't exactly expecting company. But the two men are distracted getting warm and urging life back into purple fingers and toes. I do what I can to tend to them.

"I saw your plane go down," I say, once their numb limbs have been brought back to life sufficiently. "It went down quick. What happened?"

"I don't know." The man with the dog scratches the russet and white husky behind the ears. "It was weird. We were totally fine, and then when we were going over the river the engine must have just failed or something. We just dropped. The plane hit the ice, but it was thinner than it should be. Part of the plane went through. Sorin here pulled me and Aspen out just before we got pulled under with it. Saved our lives."

"Weird," I echo.

"Yeah," says the pilot. "I've never seen the ice that thin. And there was running water in patches. More than I've ever seen this time of year."

"I suppose we should introduce ourselves," the man at the table says. "I'm Sorin Von Brandt."

He extends a hand, still colder than it should be. It's a deathly pallor against my olive-bronze skin.

"Senka Tar- Senka Samson," I say. "I work here at the outpost."

"Skeleton crew?" Sorin asks.

"You could say that." I don't know that I want to lead with how no one will notice my murder until well after it happens. That only Aguta or McGill would come looking before sunrise at the end of January. That the deer freezer behind me could easily store a body.

"And you are?" I turn to the pilot.

"Oh, sorry." He playfully ruffles the husky's fur. "I'm Finn. Finn Osborn. This is Aspen. She's my copilot." Aspen paws him, seeking attention or reassurance. "Mr. Von Brandt had a problem at a drilling site he needed to get to."

"I work for Midnight Oil," Sorin explains.

"He's being modest. He basically owns Midnight Oil," says Finn. "It's been in the Von Brandt family for generations. Old Man Norman said he's the spitting image of his uncle, Aleksandr, at his age."

"He was taller," Sorin insists.

I try to remember my manners as my guests settle in. We try the radio, but it's out. Sorin says it must be the interference from the storm. The snow has started in earnest now. He and Finn will just have to sit tight as the storm bears down on us. We'll get help after it passes.

I make us some real food. Grilled ptarmigan and potatoes. I even break out the akutaq for a real Alaskan treat. We get to talking.

"You from here?" I ask Finn.

"I'm not really from anywhere. Mom was a bit of a gypsy, so we never stayed too long in one place."

I try to keep my face neutral, but Sorin notes the twitch.

"Anyway, I got stationed here," Finn continues between eager bites. "When I got out of the Air Force I stayed. My fiancé and I are trying to save up enough to build a house."

He reaches into his pocket and pulls out his wallet. Inside

is a picture he hands me. It's a pretty black woman with a self-conscious grin but smiling eyes. She's probably around my age, maybe a little older.

"She's beautiful," I say.

"Her name's Sarah." He beams. "We have the plans for the house. Solar panels. Industrial grade greenhouse. Even a goat pen with a heated floor. Total off-grid and sustainable. It's our dream. We both want the homesteader life for our kids. At least the option of it. And with everything going on in the world..."

Sorin makes a noise of agreement.

"Anyway, we've been saving all our Alaska Dividends and as much of our paychecks as we can and we finally have enough. Come spring, we'll be breaking ground." Finn looks triumphant as a cattle dog that's just scared a wolf off the herd. He frowns. "My plane might set me back a bit, though."

Sorin is silent.

Finn raises his glass of Ovaltine. "To a fallen friend. Zephyr and I had a lot of close shaves together and I could always count on her." Until he couldn't.

"To Zephyr," Sorin and I salute.

The conversation changes. Planes. The oddly warm fall we had (Sorin still insists that cold is cold). Run-ins with moose. Outhouse horror stories. The price of oil. Sarah again.

Sorin expresses concern for their kids. Not a lot of black kids running around Alaska. Sarah grew up here, Finn tells us. But Sarah's brother is lighter skinned. Sometimes people assume she was adopted.

"Same when I visit my sister," I say. "Everyone thinks we mean we're close like sisters. But we can mock them in Romani to their faces, so, y'know, it's the simple joys." I take a sip and warmth spreads through my chest. "It makes awkward subway rides much more fun."

"Romani?" Finn asks. "Like Romanian?"

"No, not like Romanian."

Finn doesn't know what I mean.

"We're Roma." I set the mug down on the floor between me and Finn. "Well, I'm half."

His face is still blank.

"She means Gypsies," Sorin says.

Something about the way he says "Gypsies" bothers me more than how Finn said it. Finn didn't mean anything by it. To him it was just a word for itinerant. He didn't know there was a cultural context.

Finn still looks confused. "Oh. Like for real? Like in Marvel?"

Now I'm the one slow to follow.

"Magneto's kids?"

"Magneto's kids." My voice is flat. "Yeah, like that."

He starts telling me about a comic book about Magneto. How he learned more about the Holocaust from it than from school. The conversation turns to more modern politics. Sorin doesn't say much, but he makes me feel uncomfortable in my skin. I try to steer us back to "neutral" topics. I feel like Mom at Thanksgiving when Mike's brothers ask if Daniela has a boyfriend yet. I feel like a coward.

The night wears on, and Finn grows tired. I can't tell anymore. I always feel drained. But some nights sleep comes easier than others. It's not like I didn't have things to worry about before. But it's different now, even so.

In my dream I see Yuka again. She and I are in school, but she's dressed like she's on a hunt. All wolf and fox pelts. It's not the school I know. Some archetypal school building I've never seen. Old-fashioned. Yuka dips a pen in an ink bottle and writes her name on the paper in front of her. Yuka.

A ruler slams down on the desk.

"Write your name," says a school marm.

Yuka, the pen scratches.

The ruler again.

"Your name," the schoolteacher repeats. Her collar and her waist are high. Her bun tight. She looks like a Little House on the Prairie character.

Mercy, the pen concedes.

"Again."

Mercy.

"Again."

Mercy.

The schoolteacher starts tearing away the pelts Yuka wears. Yuka is screaming. I'm shouting. My own form melts away, and now I'm a wolf. I lunge at the teacher, but she changes.

She has a clipboard now. Looks like a government worker. I'm in a cage. There's a light in my eyes. Like the ones at the dentist or in an operating room. I pace on four legs.

The woman grabs my paw through the bars and inspects it. She measures my snout. My fangs. I try to pull away. She makes notes and tucks the pencil behind her ear.

The classroom melts away. The Northern Lights are above me now. A helicopter thrums over me, cutting through the aurora, breaking up the dance. A man in a hat like Finn's leans out. He has a gun.

My paws carry me as fast as I can. I try to outrace death.

A figure grabs me. It tears at my own wolfskin. I fall to the ground, just a woman. I look up and see the face of a man. It keeps changing. Sorin. The man at the diner in Barrow when I visited Yuka last. The man on the subway who wouldn't leave Daniela and her girlfriend alone. The tourist at the airport who took my father's picture. Even McGill.

A streak in the sky. A plane going down. Or a falling star. Finn is falling. He burns in the wreckage, slips beneath the ice.

Sarah screams, holding their children to her. They turn

into refugees like I see on the news in high definition. Like my grandmother's one surviving family photo. Faded and yellowed.

I wake up with my heart pounding.

PART IV - STORMFRONT

I tell myself I'm okay. It's all okay. I'm safe. Yuka is safe. Daniela is safe. It'll be okay. But I don't believe it.

Something isn't right. I feel it in my bones. The way my grandmother felt a storm before it hit. You always think a storm is coming, my mother would say. But eventually my grandmother was always right.

Outside the blizzard has intensified. Snow drifts pile high and then blow away in the wind, scattered, revealing whatever was buried under the sea of blinding white.

I pace my little world in the dark. My feet know the way. My eyes adjust.

I hear a noise in the room beyond. The one where I store supplies. The one Finn and Sorin are bunked down in, in the old musty sleeping bags left from whomever had this post before me. Maybe the one before him.

My heart hammers in my throat. I push open the door as quietly as I can. In the dark I only see one lump in a sleeping bag. I hear moans. Like a wounded animal.

I fumble for the pull chain. The old lightbulb takes a moment to get the signal. Dimming light fills the room as I pray the bulb won't burn out now. It flickers like a strobe light.

Finn's sleeping bag is soaked in blood. He's pale as death. He whimpers like a cub, tries to reach a hand out. His fingers twitch. I want to go to him, but I hear a noise again. I hear voices.

Dread douses me like ice water. Like kerosene. Sorin. On

the radio.

A ghost, I leave the threshold of the storage room. I make my way back to the main room. As close as I dare. I crouch by the deer freezer, but the computer and the radio are fixed in my sights. I can see Sorin bent over it, his figure gaunt in the shadows.

I freeze. Try not to make a sound. Try to listen; to make sense of what's happening. It's all so sudden and overwhelming. I'm still waking up.

"...plane went down," he says. "The pilot got injured in the crash. Lost a lot of blood. I carried him to the outpost, but he didn't make it."

"Liar!" I scream.

Wolfskin crackles over me as I leap, still in the dark but beginning to see. Sorin catches wolf-me in the chest and swats me aside like it's effortless. The wind is knocked out of me. I'm a woman again. Just like in the dream.

"A werewolf," he says. "How exotic."

I can't see his lips move in the dark, but somehow I know he's grinning.

"Finn may be too trusting of strangers, but where I come from we never forgot your kind," he spits. "We always knew monsters were still out there, waiting to find their way in."

"My people have monsters too," I say, rising. "We call them Upyri. Strigoi. Vurdalak."

"Vampire?" He chuckles softly. "I admit it. Why not? I'm proud of what I am."

"So am I," I growl.

I hear something outside. He's put Aspen out in the cold. She cries in desperation and fear, afraid for someone she cannot help. Someone she was supposed to protect.

I hear the radio crackle.

"Hello? Hello?" Aguta's voice fills the dark. "Sorin? Senka? Senka, if you're there...." It cuts in and out, weak against the

worsening storm. "...and Lusa. They're dead. Bled to death....
and even Old Man Norman's.... not sure.... looking... think
he... also... hospital in... row..."

I rush Sorin for the radio, catching him by surprise with my
own strength. He grabs at me with pale fingers, but I fumble,
trying to reach. My hands close around the cool plastic, my
lifeline to the world.

"Aguta!" I shout. "Aguta, send help! Sorin's lying! He
murdered Finn. He's a monster. A murderer! Help!"

Sorin seizes the radio. The signal goes dead and he
smashes it down on me. I cry out, try to get away. I bolt for
the entryway, for the door. I have to force it open against the
drift built up against it. An arctic wind cuts into the building.
Snow spills over the threshold of my former shelter.

Sorin is on me again. My fingers claw at the doorframe,
trying to hold on. He pulls me back, dragging me. He bumps
a tin of mementos on my desk. They spill everywhere.

I grasp blindly for something. Anything. My bloodied
fingers close around a familiar shape. A sewing needle carved
from bone. My father's mother's. I strike back wildly, unsure
where to aim.

Sorin snarls and pins me down. A pressure on my chest.
My heart beats fast. I feel the vein throbbing in my temple. In
my neck. Something cracks. I scream.

Sorin is screaming now. The pressure is gone. I roll free.
Aspen is on Sorin. Jaws clamped around his leg. He swears
and hits her. Aspen squeaks.

I grab a lantern, fumbling in the dark. Feel for matches on
my desk. I strike one and a small light illuminates some of
the dark. Sorin flails for it. The lantern smashes to the floor.
Fire catches.

Sorin and I struggle. His clothes catch light. He shrieks and
tries to stamp it out, smothering the flame before it spreads
and the whole outpost goes up in a blaze of old wiring and

oil drums.

The lantern, now righted, still burns against the cold. It reflects in Aspen's eyes like the sun's bright flame on the distant face of the moon. Aspen's teeth are bared, daggers of pearl in the orange glow. She's hurt still. But she isn't alone now.

A wolf and a dog block Sorin from his way out. He's alone. Not me. Aspen doesn't know me, but she's loyal and good and she knows Sorin is a shared enemy. I raise my voice. A war cry, a rally. Aspen's voice joins mine.

Somewhere far away, others hear me. They must. Foxes maybe. Other wolves perhaps. Maybe a bear.

Our last stand here under the polar night. The land may have changed these 12,000 years. There may be new faces, new tongues, new evils. But my father's people are still here. My mother's family came and lived and died here.

I'm here. This is my home. This is my land too. And men like Sorin have taken enough.

I smell fear. If I weren't a wolf, I'd smile.

Sorin tries to get past us and stumbles against the wall. His arm catches the switch, and light floods the room. He can see the shadows for what they are now. And it scares him more. He looks around for comfort, but sees only himself in the metallic surface of the deer freezer nearby. His face changes. The illusion falls away. He's a shapechanger too. An illusionist.

Where once he had the unnerving beauty of a Victorian death mask, he now grows bulbous and bloated. His frame slumps, not at all the gallant image he projected. He looks more like a dying man than something immortal or some ancient greatness risen from the dead.

His face is ruddy, an ill-boding color mottled over with pockmarks and broken capillaries. His neck is thick, his jowls like melting wax. It looks like liver failure would do him in faster than a stake to the heart. His hair greys, greasy and hanging in limp strings over his bloodshot eyes.

The poster boy of imagined Viking-esque looks is gone. Only the truth remains. A man grown soft and fat on the blood of others. With only a sham of nobility and strength to the identity he claims. It's a distortion, a corruption.

I bare my teeth, a low growl in my chest. My heart beats, a steady drum even with the bones he fractured. Aspen advances.

He runs, pushes past us. Once over the threshold, he trips. Crawling through the snow till he finds his feet. His would-be monsters at his heels, he makes for safety. But all there is is white and flat. Snow is coming down on him hard. He's blinded. He shields his eyes as the snow stings and the wind burns.

He doesn't know this land, not really. His drills may have torn into it, but it isn't his. It was just a thing to own. To use. Not a place to know, to make a life, to give back to. He doesn't know it like me. Like Sarah. Like Finn.

He runs faster and farther than he should really be able to by the looks of him. But Aspen and I could run all night.

The snow has covered the world. Everything looks the same. But it's an illusion. He doesn't realize the ground beneath his feet has changed. It isn't nearly as solid as he thinks.

Something cracks. Gives way beneath him. A burden finally heavy enough for it to break through, even after the snow piled up all this time with only a groan of protest, ignored. The vampire curses his last. He falls through the thinning sea ice.

The arctic waters swallow him up.

I cradle the body of Finn Osborn. A trail of blood shows where I had to drag him past the threshold and through the

snow. Aspen howls beside me. A blood-stained picture of
Sarah is crumpled in Finn's death grip.

The storm has broken. This one at least. I know there will
be more before the sun rises and the winter ends. I pray for
Aguta to arrive with the plane. To take Finn's body. To take
me to the hospital in Barrow.

The radio lies in plastic shards and metal scraps on my
floor, but I e-mailed her. McGill was supposed to be back by
now, but he's missing too. So Aguta is coming. I cleared the
snow for her. The weather is with us. I just have to wait.

Somewhere just beyond the edge of the world, I know
there is a dawn. A tomorrow I don't yet know. A future that
may yet hold anything. My memories may yet fade, an old
photo bleaching away like my bones one day will. Buried and
eventually uncovered by time or shifting landscapes.

But I still see the darkness all around me. And I know that
any dawn is still a long way off. I can still smell the blood,
much as the snow covers it. I can still hear my heart pounding,
an echo in my ears.

I know what happened in the night, in the shadows some of
us cling to as armor and some of us would rather forget, lest
they weigh too heavily upon us or let us grow accustomed to
the dark. I know what I have survived and what my ancestors
endured. It all runs together like a grandmother's stories, like
blood.

We fear the wolf because it's easier than admitting the
truth. *We* let the vampire in. Because we were scared. Because
we were weak. Because we feared something else more than
the devil we knew. Then we claim we didn't know.

We say we'll never let it happen again, an easy oath to make
when the sun rises. But when night falls, we fear what we see
in the shadows or imagine we see. We want the shadows gone
again.

But there have always been shadows. There will always be

shadows. And we will always see what we fear most in them, as long as we fear to turn a light on the truth, to flood the room with a harsh glare we'd rather look away from than risk having our own deeds reflected back at us. We shield our eyes, afraid of what we'll see. What we already know, somewhere deep in our bones.

They'll be there so long as we forget what we've done and what we might do again. When the monsters become real to us once more and our neighbors look more like strangers. What we say we would never be capable of, never even consider. Until we do. For shadows are no small thing here.

PREY
SARAH BIGHAM

Sarah Bigham teaches, writes, and paints in Maryland where she lives with her kind chemist wife, their three independent cats, an unwieldy herb garden, several chronic pain conditions, and near-constant outrage at the general state of the world tempered with love for those doing their best to make a difference. A Pushcart nominee, her poetry, fiction, and nonfiction have appeared in Bacopa, descant, indicia, The Quotable, Rabbit, Serving House Journal, Touch, *and other great places for readers and writers. Find her at www.sgbigham.com.*

Hunted and trapped
Poisoned and stabbed

Feared and loathed
Scorned and abused

And yet the wolf
Returns again   and again   and again   and again

Tenacity and majesty
The king reclaims his place

Now justice demands that
We become the prey

COLLAGE
KERSTEN CHRISTIANSON

Kersten Christianson is a raven-watching, moon-gazing, high school English-teaching Alaskan. When not exploring the summer lands and dark winter of the Yukon Territory, she lives in Sitka, Alaska with her husband and photographer Bruce Christianson, and daughter Rie. She completed her MFA in Creative Writing/ Poetry through the University of Alaska Anchorage (2016).   Her book of poetry Something Yet to Be Named *published by Aldrich Press is forthcoming (2017).*

First, a layer of Gesso
to cover the old hurts,
the stories gone awry,
run amok into the woods.

Next, the array of papers:
patterned, foiled, stamped.
Words surface: *Serendipity.*
List of illustrations. Her.

So like the tiny cabin
on the bluff of a northern
inlet. At times, masked
in alpenglow; sometimes

washed and warmed by long
afternoon sun. Next, gathered
from scraps, paper-rolled beads,
découpaged, tied with a silver

thread of secrets. The line
of river dividing forest and shore.
Here the gray wolf emerges
from a brood of bare branch

trees, shadowed in a stained
glass sky. With curious gaze,
scans the perimeter, considers
the border of her canvas.

WE HAVE A LOT TO LEARN
LINDA M. CRATE

Linda M. Crate is a Pennsylvanian native born in Pittsburgh yet raised in the rural town of Conneautville. Her poetry, short stories, articles, and reviews have been published in a myriad of magazines both online and in print. She has three published chapbooks A Mermaid Crashing Into Dawn *(Fowlpox Press - June 2013),* Less Than A Man *(The Camel Saloon - January 2014), and* If Tomorrow Never Comes (Scars Publications, *August 2016). Her fantasy novel* Blood & Magic *was published in March 2015. The second novel of this series* Dragons & Magic *was published in October 2015. The third of the seven book series* Centaurs & Magic *was published November 2016. Her novel* Corvids & Magic *was published March 2017.*

My cousin's dog
was part-wolf
large and white
beautiful as any
wolf of the wild
I could not help but be intrigued,
and he was a gentle giant
letting me pet him;
and licking my hands through the
enclosure that fourth of July
he barked and fussed at me
when I left to join my family for dinner—
sweet as sugar,
and more compassionate than
some of the humans I have ever known
he reminded me that every wild thing
only wants to know a gentle
touch,
and to feel loved in some capacity;
they may not understand us but I don't think we
fathom them either—
we consider ourselves a superior species,
but in the end, we are animals, too;

we have a lot to learn.

The Night Dreamer
Ann Crystal

Ann Crystal is a self-published poet, writer, and artist who lives in Los Angeles, California. She has been writing and drawing since her elementary years, with many of her works centered on the genres of fantasy and supernatural. Ann Crystal is a fourth-generation Californian, with a maternal lineage from the Tohono O'odham Natives of Arizona. Ann Crystal's work often has elements of environmental awareness and sometimes religious highlights from her Catholic upbringing.

I am a lone wolf,
one who sleeps away the day,
because it pains me to see,
what the light of the sun reveals.
The night is when I wander,
when I can visualize what once was.
Each night I make the journey,
I climb to the top of a hill.
The creeks are dried,
all the trees have been cleared,
but this is not what I see.
My eyes view a reality that is a dream,
a dream of what once was.
I run alongside my pack,
lead by my alpha,
through our woods,
a forest alive and well.
You can hear my howl,
each and every night,
once I make it,
to the top of that hill.
Where I rest,
and visualize the way it once was,

until the light of dawn,
sends it all away.
Then I journey back down the hill,
to sleep away the day,
because the night is when I live,
the dream of what once was.

DEN MOTHER
TIMOTHY DUTTON
For Sylvia

Tim is originally from Birmingham, England and grew up as part of a small family. He now has a family of his own and works as an engineer on marine craft. An avid music and literature lover, occasionally plays guitar (badly) and sings (even worse).This is his first venture into the world of published writing which was inspired by the death of a relative. He hopes you enjoy his words.

As den mother
She watched and waited,
Sitting poised
Breath bated,
As the pack grew
And slowly abated,
Seeing and knowing all

Through thick and thin
She raised the pack,
Showering praise
She took no flack,
Though members left
They all came back,
Heeding den mothers call

As all the pups knew
Den mother was right,
Until upon
A peaceful night,
She slowly faded
Out of sight,
From the dark
To rest forever,
in the light.

Keeper of Balance
Christian Esche

Christian was born on the 17th of June in Chemnitz, Germany. Ever since then, he has had a passion for drawing, and there was rarely a sheet of paper that wasn't at least doodled on, often to the dismay of his teachers. However, he never ceased drawing, and in 2015, when he was already studying at University, he began to draw digitally, which opened many new ways for his creative work. After school, he began to study Culture in his hometown, yet he wasn't suited for entirely theoretical work to say the least and finally, in 2017 he was accepted at an art school and was given the chance to make more of his lifelong passion than just a hobby and it surely was a big step for him. Beginning in October 2017, he will study Multimedia and Virtual Reality Design in Halle, Germany.

One
Christian Esche

CORA DENS WITH WOLVES
KATE FALVEY

Kate Falvey is the author of The Language of Little Girls (David Robert Books), a poetry collection, as well as the chapbooks, What the Sea Washes Up (Dancing Girl Press) and Morning Constitutional in Sunhat and Bolero (Green Fuse Poetic Arts). Her poetry has been widely published in an eclectic variety of journals and anthologies. She has also published fiction, work for children, and scholarly articles, primarily on women writers. She is the editor- in- chief of the 2 Bridges Review, published through the New York City College of Technology of the City University of New York, where she teaches. She also serves as an associate editor for N.Y.U. Langone Medical Center's Bellevue Literary Review.

She didn't last long on the trail
with its rocky switchbacks and
angular maws gaping
from the unresponsive trees.
No help for the weary in the skinny
wend of bird cry or the sneak of those hairy
runners slinking weak greens across the uphill.
This wasn't the dainty lark she'd reckoned on,
full of campion and clover, fairyslipper, shooting star
pinking damply in the early purl of sun,
the wise earth coddling her climb,
the allied air wafting her on a current of sweet avowal.

Instead there is impossible fog banked with beaks
and cold dominion and too many churlish stumbles
for her to feel dryadically inclined.
She tries to imagine her feet shod in
actual fairy slippers and her leafy hair
haloed in the poison of an amanita cap
worn to confound the bosky spring of claws
and ordinary instincts.
Loons stretch their spooky tongues

into the darkening clutch of mist, their watery
insistence unearthly, unexpected. She tilts

in their direction, hears the scratch of what
surely are not loons grabbling sharply on the granite
shears and close enough to halt her
in her semi-shambling tracks. The fog is thick
but she knows there can't be loons
so far from lakes. So what else howls and cross-
howls in mystic conversation
and patters in the pall of woodsy elevation?
Wild dogs? Dingoes are Australian, she believes.
Foxes are too scrawny to be heard and do they yip
with such duration? Absurdly, she's relieved,
until seized with recognition and a galvanizing dread.

She'll never fully know how she sped and leapt
with fleet precision down the steeply fogbound
slope until she lit on habitation and then stopped
to still her heart and steel her nerve for taking stock.
At night, denned in furry throw and pallid fleecy shawl,
she bays into the eiderdown, testing primal howls.
She moons about proximity, carrion, divinity,
tooth and claw and mystery, near misses, mossy clarity,
and accidental sanctuary while a spiral of jackdaws
muzzle golden eyes into her dreams and a miracle
of feral invitation lulls her into wilder visioning.

A Tale of Two Wolves
Richelle Gardner

Richelle Gardner is a 17 year old from a small town in NY called Downsville. She's going into her senior year of high school and studying to be a vet, she's already gotten her NOCTI and CVA level 1. She couldn't have done her artwork "Tale of Two Wolves," which is what the text written on the piece says in Cherokee, without the help of her art teacher, Mrs. Wilbur and English teacher, Mr. Morris, who are always encouraging her to think outside the box and use what she has to make something even greater. She can't really put into words how much she appreciates everything they do for her, and she can only hope that she can pass on all they've taught to others. Also, it was a little Cherokee prayer that inspired her to draw this

LYCANTHROPOTHERAPY
JAIME U. GONZALEZ

Jaime Gonzalez holds a Bachelor of Arts in English and Bachelor of Science in Criminal Justice Administration because why not? He attended Middle Tennessee State University to prove they take anybody these days. Jaime has worked as a script consultant, as an editor for numerous refugee advocacy publications, and as a part-time bear wrestling coach. He continues to balance work with education. When Jaime is not busy losing sleep or screaming himself to sleep in front of a computer monitor, he can be found singing R&B hits from the 90s to the coolers in the frozen foods section at two a.m. because they listen to anybody these days.

Dr. Elise Withers showered flakes into the tank.

"One, two, three, four," she said as greedy fish soared up to the surface, snatching and gulping up the grub. "Five— hmm." She looked into the tiny castle. That's where at least one or two of her half-dozen little *sharks* liked to hide out every now and then.

"Sylvia," she said, staring at the floating silhouette in the portcullis. "You better get some din-din before it's all gone."

"I think her babies are ready to hatch," said Ms. Teresa, taking down some of the outdated books from Elise's shelf. Old DSMs, bulky psychology books from college, and a copy of Carl Jung's *The Undiscovered Self.* Elise had not wanted to do it herself., the housekeeping. There was a photograph on the shelf that she had been avoiding. The girl in it was holding the books for her first day of first grade. She had called it *big kids' school.* Now she guarded the shelf, andightning shot into Elise's heart every time she looked at the photo by accident.

The fish had nearly gobbled everything up before Elise put one more shake in for good measure.

"I'll check on her again before I leave." She capped the fish food and slid it back into the lamp table drawer.

"Sweetie I don't think your 5 o'clock is going to show," said Teresa.

"It's alright," Elise said, clearing off her desk. Her hand bumped a Chicago Bears bobble head. "I'll give him about another ten minutes. You should get on home. Heard it's going to drop down into the teens tonight."

"13 degrees, yes ma'am," Teresa said as she carried a box full of books into the reception room. Ms. Teresa was a southern woman. She had moved with her husband and two daughters up to Chicago some thirty years ago. Elise was half Ms. Teresa's age. Yet for Elise, the weight of the city at times seemed to bear down on her like an overturned trailer skidding across an icy highway. Ms. Teresa never seemed to stress out over anything. She always had some sage southernism that she delivered with her adorable drawl.

"Well I don't want you staying here all by your lonesome with him if he does show."

"I'll be fine," Elise said, putting her hair into a ponytail with a brooch shaped like a conch. Abby had bought it for her. It was the last thing Abby ever bought.

"I got this Teresa. It's fine. Just leave the disclosures on top of the chart. I'll get him to fill everything out."

"Alright then sweetheart. But if you need me for anything—"

"Holler I will, Ms. Teresa. Have a good night."

"You too, darling," Elise heard her scoop up her purse and click her computer monitor off. "Don't stay too late now."

"I won't," said Elise as the door chime sounded.

And then there was silence. Teresa had been gone only a few minutes before Elise got that old familiar feeling. It's a quiet liquid that floods your heart, filling all the spaces where your love and faith used to be. She had become so neurotic, so OCD about it all that she kept moving Abby's picture away from the desk. The edge of the desk was safe at first. Then Elise remembered when Abby used to rest her chin on that part of the desk knowing mommy had strawberry candy in the letter drawer. Knowing that if she whimpered long enough like a puppy mommy would give her some.

Then the lamp table was home to Abby's photo, but Elise remembered that was where Abby did her adding and subtracting. She had said the light helped her think. The bookshelf became the only place where the photo was safe. Safe for Elise. Away from mommy's important work. Elise ached for Abby, but work kept mommy busy, distracted. The Head Doctor, in all her study, in all eleven years of clutching at minds, in all the treatments she rendered, could not bring herself to look at that smile. Those eyes. That picture hurt her. So work became the recommended treatment. Her prolonged, raw therapy.

"Glen Flickman," Elise opened the flaps to 5 o'clock's chart. "Get the lead out, Glen."

She kicked off her flats and curled up into her favorite of the two therapy chairs. It seemed softer than the other one, though they were identical. She checked her watch – 5:07

Three more minutes she thought. *Then you'll have to reschedule, Flickman.*

The rest of the chart was missing most of his personal information. Teresa was usually good at getting patients to forward their medical records from their previous doctors, but Glen's chart was almost empty. Aside from his name and phone number it had no identifying information. Even the referring physician slot was blank. It stated flatly: court ordered. Elise could not remember clearing any court ordered client with Teresa. Then again, Judge Hatcher did have a habit of calling Teresa directly. Once he had even sentenced a supervising manager from some sporting goods store to therapy without actually informing Teresa or Elise. Teresa had no idea who he was when he showed up, and he nearly had a meltdown in front of two clients sitting silently in the waiting room.

Elise looked over at the fish tank. They had all fled to the refuge of the sunken castle.

I wonder if they can feel each other in there. Keep each other warm.

Elise checked her watch again – 5:10. She slapped the chart shut. Her patience had run out when she heard the door chime.

"Shit," she said under her breath.

"Give me just one second."

Elise stacked the forms onto the clipboard and slipped her feet back into her shoes.

Still thinking of you, Abby.

Elise heard someone sniffing in the waiting room.

"Sorry I'm late, Doc," a man's voice said.

"Be right there."

Hefting herself up from the warmth of her chair, she walked to the door. When she opened it she saw a somewhat tall man standing by the reception desk. His face was hidden from view as his back was turned to Elise. He wore a dark leather coat and on his head he had a large toboggan. The kind that usually had a bill in the front and generous flaps draped over the ears.

"Glen."

"Panic button."

"What?"

"Do you have a panic button?"

"Yes, Glen," she said, thinking she might actually have to use it in about two and half seconds. That's not a normal question for a client to ask. The average person would not even know to ask that sort of thing. This was someone who had either been in and out of therapy, or someone who had the button used on them.

"Do you need help?" asked Elise.

"Just hear me out," he said. "I'm going to turn around. Please, try not to freak out and run to the button when you see my face. Give me a chance to—explain things and well—you'll see."

Nobody's told me not to freak out since I decided to go to grad school, she thought.

"Okay, Glen. I promise, but how about you tell me why I don't need to freak out,"she said.

Elise felt her muscles tense, her feet primed. Twice since moving to this clinic had Elise ever had to plunge that red button, and both times had been on accident. She did not want a real reason to use it. Not tonight. Not now.

As Glen turned around Elise thought she could see frostbite on the tip of his nose, but when more of his face came into view she realized it was not trauma at all. The shiny black tip became a gray, whiskered muzzle. Fiery yellow orbs with dark halos were nested beneath bushy brows. And then all Elise could see were the massive hook-like teeth sticking out of it's mouth. Her stomach turned to ice.

Panic button, NOW.

She swung the door closed, but Glen caught the door jamb with a furry hand.

"Ow," he whimpered. "Dr. Withers, wait."

Elise felt her heart skip a beat. Her chest tightened up as she sucked in her breath.

"Mommy I hope you never have to use it but," Abby's voice echoed in Elise's head.

The voice sounded so clear. So present. That night Abby had been learning her multiplication tables beneath the lamplight.

"You might have to run one day. You can't run good without shoes mommy."

Abby had never liked it when Elise would walk around the office without shoes. Elise never thought she would have to sprint in her own office, but since the talk, she chose to take her daughter's advice. The night Glen showed up she was grateful for that much.

Elise felt the shoe treads grip the rug, catapulting every cell in her body towards the red button just beneath her stationery drawer.

"Doc listen to me for a sec," Elise heard a voice say.

She could hear everything, see everything, but nothing could be appreciated, accepted. The only thing that mattered—

Panic button, NOW.

She was passing the lamp table. Not less than three feet away from her desk she heard footsteps thump across the rug. It was Glen. He had crossed the room in half the time it took Elise. She half expected to catch a musty wave of sweat and stink, but instead she caught a whiff of Old Spice and the faint odor of a mild cologne coming from Glen's wall of a chest. Still, it did not matter. She was shoving away her chair and lunging for the button when she heard the voice again.

"Don't be afraid," Glen blurted. When Elise looked up he was standing in front of her desk with a guilty glaze in his eyes.

He looks like he just broke something, she thought.

Elise lifted the clear cover, but she stopped herself before slamming down on the red disk.

"Time out Doc," he said. "I know this is super weird."

Something is broken.

"But you did promise not to freak."

Her heart was still pounding. Beads of sweat streamed down her hot cheeks.

"Wha-wha-what," her throat felt dry and still as she forced out the words. "What are you?"

"I'm Glen."

He bared his teeth in what Elise could only guess was his smile.

"So, okay, I know this is a lot for you," he said, taking off his toboggan. A pair of gray ears pointed straight up toward the ceiling.

"The moral of the story is," he said. "Don't put on an eighteen hundred year old wolfskin from the Teutoborg forest."

Glen was shaking. For a moment, Elise thought she might start to feel some actual sympathy for him.

"Even if someone bets you a hundred bucks that you won't."

And then that moment was gone.

"You're 1800 years old?"

"What? No. God, no. Had an old buddy from college whose dad was an appraiser, and he nabbed this ancient wolf pelt from some dying Russian mobster who was trying to sell it on the black market. But what ended up happening wa--"

"Whoa, whoa. Glen you are going to need to slow down, alright."

"Doc I wish I had an easier way of putting it, but I don't," Glen's wooly hands peeled off his coat. Tufts of dark gray fur stuck out from the sleeves of his sweater.

"Glen this looks serious."

Glen erupted into spasms of laughter until he saw that Elise was not laughing.

"Oh, sorry. I, uh," his ears cowed down. He looked embarrassed, disarmed.

"I guess that's the nice way of putting it."

He plopped himself into the same leather therapy chair Elise had been sitting in earlier.

"I made assistant DA when I was 24," he said with a distant smile on his face. "Hustling. Closing. Convicting. They started calling me the Blur. Things couldn't have been better. Rachel, my girl. We started talking plans. After about a year at the DA, I was starting to save up some cash, so I put a down payment on a ring. I had a four day weekend coming up, so we decided to go see my friend Derek in Rochester. I was going to pop the question to Rachel when we got back. See I knew she was going to be expecting it to happen when we were out of town but I—I made her wait."

Glen was miles away.

"I shouldn't have done that."

Elise could barely hear his voice above the soft hum from the fish tank.

"We were all in his the trophy room. Derek brought out this pelt. It was black and—and old. I don't think I'd ever seen anything that old before. He bet me I wouldn't do it. I screwed up Doc."

Glen was no longer looking at Elise but through her. She had seen that look before. More times than she cared to remember.

"When I put it on I saw things Doc. Things I know couldn't be real. Things that couldn't—didn't happen to me, but I knew I was—I was remembering it all. As if it did. I took it off and pretended like nothing happened. When I opened my eyes, I was in the trophy room again, but I wasn't."

Glen's eyes rose to meet Elise.

"The blackouts came first. I was missing work. Showing up and leaving at weird times. Forgetting client meetings, entire cases. Rachel was trying to figure out what was going on. Then there was the fur in the shower and in the bed. Rachel thought I was losing my hair. She didn't know what was going on. I didn't know what was going on. Doc, I love her, but I didn't know what to say to her."

Elise was trying to remember what it was like to fall in love. When she lost Abby, she had thought that Michael would stay. It was what he swore to her before all their friends, their loved ones, their unborn daughter. It was not enough. It was work to carry out their love, but after a while it felt like Elise was alone with all that weight. They started sleeping in different rooms. Talking to each other became a chore. Even eating together became a silent cold ritual. Shadows of two people scraping necessary food into their mouths. Elise sensed Michael growing more disgusted, more distrustful of their failed love because of what she was sensing in herself. Numbness set in soon after, and it never went away, even when the divorce was finalized.

You don't know a thing about love, Flickman.

It was not that Elise could not help Glen. She simply had no desire to.

"By the time I was ready to get help, Rachel was packing her bags," Glen said. "I'm trying to figure out who I am," he choked out his words.

"I feel it all the time now. This unstoppable need to run out into the wild and be free, and the memories. They—they never stop." He sighed. Some other side of Glen struggled to break loose.

"Every full moon. At least once a month I turn into—"

"A monster."

"Ouch. Try lycanthrope, Doc."

"Sorry I just... This is new for me."

"You're doing better than most."

"How did you get here?"

"Uber."

"No I mean," she said, shaking her head. "How did nobody see you?"

"It's not exactly hard to blend into a city full of people who suck at making eye contact. I got spotted by a courier once. He just said 'yup.' Got on his bike and rode away."

Elise lowered the cover back over the button. She pulled her chair back to the desk, never letting her eyes stray far away from him.

"Glen, I would be happy to initiate the consult. It's just that," she peered into her bag of convincing excuses. "You did get here rather late. I think we are just going to have to reschedule."

"Don't make me walk out of here with all this baggage, Doc."

"It's fine if you call me Dr. Withers," she said tersely.

"You know, I could actually recommend a couple of specialists who might be able to give you a more streamlined form of therapy."

"But you are the one I want to see," he said, straightening himself up in the chair.

"I came to you because I thought you'd be able to help me. I'll be honest Dr. Withers, I shopped around. All signs keep pointing to you. Plus, your Yelp reviews are really solid."

"I'm honored you think that, Glen, really," Elise reached further into the bag. "But I'm not going to be taking new clients at this time."

"I won't say nothing if you don't," he pointed to his face. "This—this isn't the worst thing about being me. That pelt is not just a fur coat or some antique or somebody's hunting trophy. It used to be a living, breathing being. I know what it saw when it was alive and free. I know the last thing that it saw."

"Glen, I'm not staffed to handle your treatment needs."

"I wish I knew what that meant."

Elise took her own seat and pulled herself to her table, majestic and professional.

"Glen, it means I don't always appreciate being scared out of my wits by a potential client."

"So I got my days mixed up and thought the new moon wasn't until tomorrow. I called this morning to reschedule, but this place is booked up until February. And if you think I'm waiting until then to get to see you, you're crazier than me."

Elise dug further.

"Glen, I need you to understand."

"Oh come on, Doc," he yelled. Elise's hand reached for the button again.

"Yeah you know what, that's fine. Press it. Everybody's got a way out, except Glen."

He shot up from the chair. His eyes scanned the bookshelf as if he was trying to summon the words to say from staring at Elise's old books.

"Once a month, I look like the three little piggies' worst nightmare. No big deal, right? Well, 365 days out of the year I'm still an animal whether I look it or not. On the inside I want to run through the forest. Every day I want to go out and find a pack of my own and forget about work. Forget about money. Forget about Rachel. Forget about this city. I don't want to be trapped inside, Doc."

"Glen, I can tell there are a number of issues you want to address," Elise had heard enough.

"But it would be best if we go ahead and set you up with another specialist. I don't think it would be appropriate if I treat you."

Elise could read the heartbreak in Glen's gray face. His eyes billowed and shook. She watched the sorrow spread over his mouth, the universality of it.

"It's fine," he said as he scooped up his coat and tossed it over his massive shoulders. "I don't want or need a different specialist. Forget it. You're probably in bigger trouble than me anyway."

"Don't try to bait me with your comments," she said. "I'm trying to be civil with you, Glen."

"It's fine if you call me Mr. Flickman," he snapped. "I may look like I just crawled out of a fairytale book to you, but I'm still living being. At best, I'll be a weird story for you to tell your friends. But I don't have any delusions about what I am. You're in way worse shape than me. At least I can admit

I need help." Elise jumped to her feet.

"You can leave now!"

"Yeah, I'm going."

"Goodnight and good-bye."

Glen turned, and made his way to the door.

"I could smell it as soon as I walked into the waiting room you know," he said. "Your sadness."

"Excuse me?"

"It's thickest in here. It'll follow you around you know, like hot flowing tar. Sticking to everything, and if you're not careful, to everyone you care about. You must think you are pretty good at hiding it from everyone."

"I am good at it, fortunately. Better than most."

"It's a bad skill be good at, Dr. Withers. Hiding what you feel all the time. How old was she?"

He saw her picture she thought. Elise burned inside. Her mouth trapped her words inside.

"I shouldn't have asked. I'm sorry for your pain," Glen said, as he lumbered toward the door.

"She was 8."

Glen stopped.

"She's got your eyes, Doc."

The air changed. It seemed cooler, calmer.

"Thank you," Elise said.

"I don't know how to stop being me." Glen said.

Elise could see his far away eyes glowing in the lamplight.

"Please. Help me get a hold of what I've got inside. Before I start digging holes in the park, burying my Chinese takeout."

You might have to run one day, Elise thought. *Just remember what to do when it's time to stop running.*

Sylvia had come out of her refuge in search of food.

"If you're not busy blowing down any little piggy homes," she said. "I might be able to squeeze you in on Monday morning."

A WOLF'S LIFE
ILONA HEGEDUS

Ilona is a Hungarian writer who lives in Budapest. She has had mainly poetry published so far in the US, UK, Greece and Hungary. Her poems have appeared in Tales of The Talisman magazine, Illumen and Universe Pathways. *She is a fan of sci-fi, fantasy, comedy and detective stories. Her blog is http://ilonasworld. blogspot.com*

When the first snow falls, we are happy
and we howl.
When men arrive, we hide.
When pups are born, we all look after them.
Then they imitate us, they copy everything
we do and they learn.
They have to know how to hunt and dig
and how to do everything else.
We have some friends in the pack, that the
alpha leads, and the omega teaches us to
play. We are all a little bit different.
When we lose a loved one, we howl.
No other animals have such a great pack
and such freedom.

HOW THE WOLVES CHANGED THE RIVER
LANA DEAN HIGHFILL

Lana Dean Highfill holds an MFA in Writing from Pacific University in Forest Grove, OR. She writes poetry in Southern Indiana, where she is an English professor. Her interests include live music, comic books, sci-fi, and marine biology. She has had poems published by Sediments Literary-Arts Journal, Slipstream Press, Lost Tower Publications, Halcyon Days Magazine, Blue Horse Press, you are here: the journal of creative geography, Three Drops Press, *and* Rose Red Review. *She is currently working on a collaborative art project for her first chapbook.*

They started out
just drinking from it,
making tiny pools
in the hollows of their jaws,
tipping their heads back
to swallow, squinting
at the dawn. They howled
from the feet of trophic
cascades, taking and giving
life, all in the same.

And the wolves, as wolves do,
changed the behaviors
of the deer, watched
the birds as they moved higher
to the newly-increased
heights of trees.

But the rivers – that's what
they changed – making the water
theirs, giving the current less desire
to meander. Like the pools in their mouths,
so formed the pools in the river, breeding
life, and life, and life.

THE CHANGE
LANA DEAN HIGHFILL

Does a werewolf get brand new skin
with each full moon? If yes,
then, oh, to be a werewolf...
to live within this shell
you so delicately caress with passion
and then to slough it off with violence
like a silk thrown to the floor: divine.

Under the skin of a werewolf
flows a blood in cycle with the sky.
Oh, to have blood with more purpose
than keeping this heart alive,
to burst forth from the stained
landscape of this body, to become
a huntress, giving song to the night.

Or does a werewolf slip back into
herself again and again, aging
as any woman does, graying
at her temples, no longer supple
to the touch? Then, no thank you.

I'll stay in this skin of mine
and save but a whisper
for the deceitful hand of the moon.

Peaceful co-existence
Diane Jackman

Diane Jackman's poetry has appeared in small press magazines and many anthologies, and it has won several competitions. Starting out as a children's writer she now concentrates on poetry. With her late composer husband, she wrote several works for choir, and in 2016, she organized a year of performances for what would have been his 70th birthday. She has just completed a sequence, Lessons from the Orchard and is now working on water poems. Her writing draws heavily on the past, and often reflects elements of magic realism.

Wolf howl
between the pines
guides our fearful footsteps
safely from vengeful pursuers
back home.

Wolf paws
in the night hours
pad around our cabin
protecting our sleep and guarding
our dreams.

Hostile
hunters with guns
silently stalk our wolf
We unlatch the door and she is
welcome.

Pain is Relative
Katja L Kaine

Katja L Kaine lives in Yorkshire, England, where she can be found roaming the countryside with her Canaan dog and creating novel writing software. She writes short stories and fantasy novels that often have strong themes tied to the natural world and the way in which humans find their place within it. You can read more of her work and rantings at www.katjalkaine.com.

The tastiest bit is the guts, like fat rubbery worms packed with treats. The sharp green smell used to make my tummy clench, but now it makes me salivate.

Mum says that's because everything is relative to how we feel about it. Taste. Hunger. Happiness. Pain.

I watch mum press her wide, rough pads to brace the hare as she tears open its skin, shaking her head and sneezing to spit out the tufts of fur.

"Eat," she says, and I fall on the juicy intestines. They taste different depending on whether the hare was last eating grass or seeds or berries. This one had berries; dry, tart ones. They're sharp on my tongue and stain the snow red. After the guts I rip off chunks of the groin, then crunch down on long thigh bones. Before I know it, I've eaten everything but the ears.

"Sorry," I say, staring at the ground.

"It's okay. Did you eat enough?"

I nod. "I'm full."

"Then I'm full too," she says. But she swallows the ears anyway, leathery and translucent.

"That doesn't make any sense," I say.

"You'll understand when you're a mother," she says, grinning at me with black lips.

If being a mother means always having to give away my food, then I'm not sure I ever want to be. But I forget about it as she shows me how to press the side of my face against the snow and push along with my back legs to clean the blood off my muzzle. The snow is crispy and makes my nose numb.

We trot back to the den. It's a very good den, tucked under a mound hidden among the trees, near the edge of the thick black forest. The smells of my older brothers and sisters are embedded in the layers of earth and leaves, so sometimes when I'm sleeping I feel like they're huddled around me, even though they live somewhere else now. Mum says that's how wolves live forever, by leaving their scent wherever they go.

Just outside the den, her nose twitches. I lift my head and puff air through my throat to try to smell what's got her attention. When I do, the whiskers on the backs of my ankles twitch.

The humans. They've moved their den again. Closer.

Mum turns and enters the den, but she's trying too hard to look like she doesn't care. She herds me to the back and starts cleaning me. It takes longer now because I'm bigger, even though I'm still only as tall as her knees. My fur has a reddish tint, and her tongue follows the patterns that look a bit like flickering rows of fire. When mum's in a good mood, she says she has to lick me all the time, or I'll start sparking and set the forest alight.

I'm sleepy by the time mum's decided I'm clean enough, but she nudges me up and out. We creep close to the human's den to spy on them.

I don't understand these animals. They can barely smell, they can't see very well, and they move so slowly. They should be as harmless as worms. But they're not at all. Because these pink grub things have somehow tamed the greatest of all beasts: fire. And they have special teeth they can spit out of their paws at great speed, like snake venom. They call these teeth *arrows*.

"Come on," says mum. "Let's go."

Now that they've moved, we're going to check out their

old den. The popup beds like tiny mountain tops they sleep in won't be there anymore, but often they leave treasures behind, like charred bones or hard, shiny slabs of leather. I find a bit of old rope tied to a thick tree root and am tugging it, growling and giving sharp jerks to try to take it by surprise, when something flies right over my muzzle. I immediately drop the rope to chase after it.

It doesn't fly for long, but bounces and rolls along the ground. I approach cautiously. It smells like pig bladder, but it's filled with human breath to make it big and round, like a summer fruit. I stalk it, shoulders rolling as I edge closer, head low. Then suddenly, there's a noise of a human behind me and I sprint for the cover of the woods, nearly tripping over my own legs.

From behind a large tree I peer out. It is a human, but it's a pup, only about half grown. It's looking at me and giggling. It walks over to the bladder, picks it up with its paw, and then tosses it towards me. I battle the urge to chase it, but it's all my body wants to do, and I can't help but bound out and pounce on it. The human squeals as my jaws close around the bladder and air starts hissing out.

There's a growl behind me. Mum, with her hackles high as porcupine spines. She stands between me and the pup, lips peeled back to display her teeth, the rumble in her throat, a message that even humans can understand.

"Go. Back to the den," she orders through her growl. "Now."

I release the bladder and run.

Back at the den my mum ignores me, gnawing at her toenails.

It's days before mum gets another kill. I should be helping by now, I'm nearly four months old. But mum says it's not my fault. It's the noise of the humans, making everything hide.

"Should we find a new den?" I ask her. "Somewhere else?"

"This was our home first," she says.

Finally, she comes back with a lizard. It's chewy and dry, but she says lizards are good for the bones. They might be good for the bones, but I'd rather have a deer. They're good for everything. Even their ridged, curving horns are good for cleaning your teeth on.

"When are we going to have a deer again?" I whine, even though I know she'll be annoyed by me asking.

"It's not a deer you want, it's an elk." She sits down on her haunches and stares out into the forest. "An elk would keep your belly stuffed all winter. The fat melts from the heat of your tongue, and the flesh is dark and rich."

"I bet the humans could kill an elk, with their arrows."

"Yes," she said. "The humans can kill anything they want." She gets up and starts padding in a tight circle, making a flat, soft spot for me to sleep.

I think of the human pup that had wanted to play with me. It reminded me of my older brothers and sisters that play with me too. They sometimes shared meat with us if they killed something big. The coyotes would steal the leftovers anyway.

"Do you think if they did, the humans would give some to us? If it was more than they needed?"

Mum ears are suddenly pointing sharply upwards. She glares at me with smoldering amber eyes. "Where would you get an idea like that?"

"Nowhere," I say, lowering my head and curling up so I can hide my face under my tail.

The next day she takes me out hunting with her, even though there's still thick snow. She has a determined set about her shoulders, and she's impatient with me as I trip in the snow that collapses under my paws.

"Step lightly," she snaps at me.

"I'm trying," I whimper, getting another face full of the

cold, wet stuff. It clogs, stinging in my nose, and muffles my smell. I can no longer sense what's around me. I feel exposed, and when she vanishes ahead of me for a moment, I instantly feel afraid.

Don't yelp, I tell myself, as the urge to cry for help builds inside me.

Suddenly, a snow rabbit explodes out of the forest. It's heading straight towards me. It sees me and twists its long legs as it lands, flinging itself off to the side, the whites of its bulging eyes showing, but it lands badly and nearly loses its balance. I leap after it, and my fear evaporates into the thrill of the chase. I snap at its toenails, frosty air against my gums, blood pumping with instant heat.

"Go, on, catch it!" I hear my mum barking encouragement. I give one last surge and close my jaws around its foot. It spasms and flings its body about like crazy, even though we both know it's over now. I suppose you don't have much choice. Even if you know you're going to die, you can't stop trying to fight it.

Mum is pleased. Her lips draw back into a grin as she trots over and sniffs the rabbit as it draws its last few breaths. It's lost too much blood to have the energy for flicking its limbs about now. Spots of blood are appearing on the snow between its yellow incisors. She licks it, and it shudders. Then it goes still.

"Eat, quickly, while it's still warm," mum says. She doesn't need to ask me twice. I swallow the rabbit in three bites as she watches me. I even eat the ears.

Mum nuzzles me, pushing firmly enough that I have to shift my balance not to topple over.

"I'm proud of you."

We go back to the den and find that the human's fires have warmed the edge of the forest and a lump of snow has fallen from an overhanging branch and slid inside through the sloping entrance. It's melting, the ground is soggy. Mum scrapes some strips of bark from trees to try to soak up the water, but soon her gums are bleeding and she can't get enough. In the end she noses as much of the bark as she can into a pile and tells me to lie on it. Then she coils herself around me like a snake, right in the water.

"Aren't you cold?" I ask. I am cozy and dry on my little island.

"I'm fine, little one," she says. She is silent for a while, then speaks softly. "There are some things that you can't live without. Like meat. And love. Then there are some things that you take when you can get, and don't worry about the rest of the time. Like berries. And being dry."

The next day some of my older brothers and sisters pass by. My mother's fur is damp, and she's shivering. There is mucus around her nose. But when I ask if she's okay, says she's fine. Nothing to worry about.

"We're going," says one of my brothers. "To the far edge of the forest. The humans aren't there."

"Good luck," says mum.

"You should come with us," he says.

"No thank you," she replies. They all look at me.

"What?" I ask. They've always been fun before, all playful bows and tug-o-war.

"She's very small," my brother say to mum. "Her chances aren't-"

"That's enough." Her fur is bristling and I feel my own fur stand up in response. "You should get going," she tells them.

They back away, keeping their eyes on her until they are a safe distance, before turning their backs and melting into the trees. As soon as they're gone, I feel lonelier. It's just me and mum now. No one to play with.

Mum is tense and still damp, and I spend a while licking her, even though the stagnant water on her fur tastes nasty.

I keep licking her until her fur is fluffed as it should again, not lying down in dark clumps. She even stops shivering, and when I start flicking my head and flapping my tongue around, trying to shake a tickly hair that's stuck in my throat, she gives a barking laugh.

She knocks me over with a head butt. I tumble down and take the opportunity to scratch my back on the ground.

"You may be small," she says, "but you are the biggest thing to me."

The winter deepens, and all but the most committed of animals give in and migrate away.

One day I can smell the humans the instant I wake up. Not their fire. Not their tempting meat over flames that makes the fat and flesh release their smells a hundredfold more intensely, but them. Actually them. Their skin, their sweat, their breath. That's how close they are.

Mum is still sleeping. She is so thin now, like a furry skin over a heap of bones. Even her nose looks thin, and it's lost its shine. Her claws are brittle and ragged. I have to do something. I have to help her. I ease myself up and away, moving slower than a mud snail. Normally I make the slightest move and she's wide awake, but she's so exhausted, she doesn't stir.

I poke my nose out and take stock. The humans have moved their den closer, it's right at the edge of the forest now, barely ten paces from the mouth of our den.

I can hear them clearly. They constantly make noise, the humans, like they don't care who might hear them. I shuffle out on my belly to the tree line. They don't notice me. They're going in and out of their mountain beds, sitting by their fires, drinking and eating.

Then I see it. The same pup I saw before. It's looking right at me. I am already still but inside I freeze. It goes to one of the fires and picks up a piece of meat. The adult humans don't pay it any attention. It comes back to me and holds out the piece of meat. I growl.

The pup flinches back a bit. Then it sets its shoulders square and shuffles even closer, then tosses the meat at me. It lands a few paces away from my nose and I let out a little whimper of desire. It's elk. I'd recognize that scent anywhere. Keeping both eyes on the pup, I rise from my belly to my feet, pad the few paces and quickly gulp it down. It tastes better than anything I've eaten in my whole life. I can taste the fire in it. I can feel it entering my bloodstream and my muscles. Only then do I remember that I was supposed to be getting some food for mum.

Humans are famous for being terrible at language, but I have to try. I angle my eyes and give a little whine from about half way down my throat.

"I'm hungry," I say in this way. "Please can I have some more?" It always works on my brothers and sisters, but on a human pup? I don't expect much.

To my surprise the pup trots back to the fire. It gets two more pieces of meat, comes back and tosses them to me. It doesn't throw so well and the pieces land a little further away, but they smell so good. I creep forward and snatch one, then go to pick up the other. I will bring it to my mother. It will be a nice waking up present for her.

Then the yelling starts.

The adult humans have seen me. Before I know it, they are pointing their arrows at me. There is a whistling sound, then a thud. Searing heat shoots through my shoulder. Warm liquid seeps from the burning agony. I stagger and collapse.

"No!" I hear my mother howl behind me. She thunders from the mouth of the den and is standing over me in an instant, her legs and body a protective shield.

More whistles, more thuds. Thick scarlet liquid makes trails down her skinny legs as they begin to tremble. I raise my head and look up at her. Arrows are sticking out of her at all angles, so she looks like a strange porcupine. Her fur is soaked with red. I can't hold my head up any more. As it flops down I see my own shoulder. An arrow. Just one. One arrow and I can barely move, but my mother is covered in them and still she stands over me, snarling like she will tear to shreds anyone who dares take a step closer. I don't understand how she can be so strong.

Then the pup runs forward. Clear liquid is running from its eyes. It stands in front of us and the adults have to stop spitting their arrows. They make angry noises, but the pup doesn't move.

I look into my mum's eyes, and they are filled with pain. But she doesn't seem to even notice the many arrows in her body. It's the one in mine that she can't take her eyes off.

She's having trouble breathing now, but she lifts her head and nudges the human pup with her nose.

"Please take care of her," she says with her eyes.

"It can't understand you, mum," I say. "It's human. Come on, we need to go." I try to get to my feet but my body is ten times heavier than it was before.

The pup's face is covered in the clear liquid now, but its eyes say 'yes'. I stare at it in surprise.

"It understood you?"

Mum's trembling legs give way and she topples down beside me. Slowly her eyes close.

I yelp, drag myself closer to her and start licking her face.

"Get up mum, come on, let's go."

"It's okay, little one. Be strong."

"No! Open your eyes!"

She obeys me, just long enough to say, "Take me with you, little one."

I inhale deeply, desperately, trying to breathe in her whole being, but it's not enough, I'm not big enough, and I can't breathe, I'm choking.

I can't feel the arrow in my shoulder anymore. It's nothing but a scratch compared to the agony that explodes from my center. I barely notice as the human pup lifts me into its arms, my soaked fur staining its chest.

Raven's Watch Twilight and Dawn
Patricia Lehtola

Patricia Lehtola is a free-lance artist whom donates her time and talent to local organizations. Her greatest inspirations are memories of the family farm in the upper peninsula of Michigan where wildlife is abundant. She currently resides in southern California with her family and Chihuahuas.

GUARDIANS OF LIGHT
PATRICIA LEHTOLA

THE NIGHT CUB
KATHLEEN LONG

Kathleen L. Long is a Medical Assistant, currently working as a Lab Technician at the Vanderbilt University School of Nursing. She is also very involved at her church as a high school youth leader. While earning her Associate Degree at Volunteer State Community College, she was a Staff Writer for the college's paper, The Settler, *and later became the Assistant Editor. She enjoys reading, writing, painting, drawing, playing instruments, doing all kinds of puzzles, Star Wars, Star Trek, superheroes, helping animals, playing video, card, and board games, and making awful short films and parody board games that have to do with her life. Her dream is to own a huge farm and have a safe place for the rehabilitation of all wildlife.*

The evening time has come upon us, and the moon is full
   in the sky.
I get ready to howl, as I do, but in an instant a dark shadow
   runs by.
Two smaller shadows follow closely behind.
I swiftly turn, trying to keep them in my line of sight.
I move in quickly, afraid of losing them in the night.

Why are they running?

I continue on the path that I think they have made.
Holding back my fears, and trying to be brave.
As the darkness sinks in more, I can't help but be afraid.
I am trying to go the correct way.
Knowing the need to follow so that I may be safe.

What are they hiding from?

I stop.
There is no more sound except for the chirping of crickets
   and frogs.
I close my eyes and listen for a clue to help me carry on.
As I am still, I suddenly have a thought.

I am lost.

When will I find them?

No friends, no warmth, no hope.
I am all alone.
So young, so afraid –my heart is turning into stone.
I accept my defeat and slowly start to roam.
With the hope that they will find me, and bring me safely
    home.

Where am I going?

I find a tree to curl up by, pondering my demise.
When suddenly I am scooped up, by a pair of dark eyes.
As I met them for a moment, I felt they were kind.
I was wrapped in warmth and held in tight.
An embrace is what I needed to give me peace of mind.

How did I get here?

It felt like so much time had passed. I breathe it through
    my lungs.
Life is now a blur, but I don't have to run.
I can't help but think, am I the only one?
Separated from my pack, my time has not yet come.
Becoming weak, but feeling safe, to know I'm not yet done.

Who has rescued me?

I awake to a familiar feeling, somewhere that I've been.
Around me and above me, I know it from within.
I open my eyes and look around, I know exactly where I
    am.

My mother is sleeping peacefully, with three cubs beneath
her chin.
Thanking whoever brought me back, instead of being
taken, to safety in my den.

They have saved me.

THE BIG RED WOLF
LEXI LONGTINE

Lexi Longtine is a not so average teenage girl on the west coast. She loves wolves with a passion and really wants to save them. She uses art to show their beauty and elegance.

WOLF OF THE FOREST
LEXI LONGTINE

LIGHT IN THE DARKNESS
LEXI LONGTINE

WHITE WOLF
MARIANNE MAGIN

Marianne A. Magin lives and works in Long Island, NY. Her interest in both art and animals started at a young age. She attended the NYS Summer School for the Arts – Visual Arts and was the recipient of the "Promising Young Artist" award from the National Foundation for the Advancement of the Arts. She has continued drawing and painting throughout her life. She currently enjoys working in watercolor on Yupo paper and doing work in pen & ink. She feels very connected to her animal subjects and is often told that she captures the "spirit or essence" of the animal she is painting. Her lifelong passion for wolves, makes her proud to be part of this anthology.

Her work can be seen at https://www.facebook.com/ArtfulPawDesigns

The Ecology of Fear
(Wolf's Story)
Tamara Miles

Tamara Miles teaches college English and Humanities in South Carolina. Her poetry has appeared in Fall Lines; O'Bheal Five Words; Love is Love; Pantheon; Tishman Review; Animal; Obra/Artifact; Not Enough to Quit; Rush; Apricity; Snapdragon; Crosswinds Poetry Journal; Whatever Our Souls, Cenacle, *and* Devil's Doorbell: Vagina Edition. *She was a 2016 contributor at the Sewanee Writers' Conference and will be in residency at Rivendell Writers Colony in August 2017.*

"I can't think of a beast that has been asked to carry more of our psychic burden than the wolf." (Jason Mark, Scientific American)

Shadowed in grey power,
in sixes and tens
beside his Alaskan brothers,
she-wolves and litters
of four or six
in dens,

the wolf knows nothing of bricks
and pigs or clocks
or riding red or leash laws
(unless we humans fence
him in, or poachers'
weapons win.)

He roams the number
of months in miles per day,
seeking elk or deer
(without him they grow lazy,
he and his family grow thin.)

With forty-two teeth
he snaps their bones; he eats,
and takes the nourishment in.

For this, his appetite,
he is hated by ranchers
whose cattle meet him
in the night.

*Canis lupus, grey wolf, western
wolf, wild timber wolf, Arctic wolf,
European wolf.*

He howls and tingles human spines ---
for this, they call him villain,

adversary, hungry ghost.
Cailleach rides upon his speeding
back.

But he also whimpers, whines,
and growls.

He speaks to the pack, his only true
divines, and they howl with him,
under moon or none.

For community, for territory,
with sound and echo, two of them
can make the sound
of four or more ---

The Beau Geste Effect,
to confuse a pack of strangers

as to their number and their size.

They know he is the first,
with his shining mate,
and separated,
their call both long and low
is lonesome.

Red wolf, southeastern
cousin, down to the last
wild one hundred.

Maned wolf,
South America, sometimes confused
for fox.

Sea wolf on the Canadian
coast.

*Mexican gray wolf, Rocky Mountain
wolf*.

Humans try to predict their fate,
but wolf knows how to wait.

You might trap him once --- but he won't
be fooled again by gun or gate.

EXTINGUISH
CAITLYN N. MLODZIK

Caitlyn N. Mlodzik is a senior at The Vanguard School in Colorado where she leads a group of aspiring young writers called Poet Society. She has had six poems published and awards for three other poems in the Scholastic Art and Writing Competition. Her work can be found in Inwood Indiana Press, The Pinyon Review, The American Library of Poetry, *and* Save the Earth Poems. *Caitlyn loves writing poetry in many different styles and on many different topics, and she strives to help fellow students share their voice in the world through their writing. When she is not writing or reading books about writing, Caitlyn enjoys photographing the oldest and greatest muse in the world: nature.*

He growls, pants, and howls,
    sending shivers down your spine,
    tipping your heart till it spills out of your chest,
    and befuddling your senses, bringing you to your knees.

Together the pack moves towards you,
    their gleaming white coats sparkling from a recent rain,
    and their mouths dripping from a recent kill.
Together the pack circles you,
    going around and around and around, till their fur blurs,
    panting and panting till their tongues seem fixed forever
    outwards.
Together the pack sniffs you,
    soaking up the darkness of your fear, your black intent,
    and extinguishing your flame, your only defense.

You freeze,
    frozen in your footsteps, frigid in your faculty.
You raise a weapon,
    rigid in your reflexes, raven dark in your ruin.
You stammer,
    stilled in your sinews, startled in your stature,
    suddenly realizing just how small you are.

One of the pack strides forward,
  a slight breeze ruffling his white fur,
and regards you with pure intensity,
  melting the meager confidence behind your eyes.
He glances at your weapon and back at you,
  questioning, though respecting your audacity.
He raises a paw slightly from the damp ground,
  water droplets falling from it and bombarding the ground.
He glances to your thick spear again,
  compelling you, almost commanding you, and you drop it.

The spear thumps the ground
  while you kneel before him, hands shaking,
  and looked straight into the wolf's icy blue eyes.
He bows his head and turns away,
  his tail high in the air and waving as if in salute,
  as the rest of the pack races after him
into the darkness of the night.

Patterns of Loudness and Softness
Caitlyn N. Mlodzik

Paws padding ever so slowly,
Surrounding you in their drums and their beats,
Challenging you with their very own timbre,
Awaiting you under cover of night.
But not to kill you,
Not to rip you to shreds.
They appear in moonlight, ever so quietly,
Growling but without malice to you,
Snarling but without threat to you,
Whining but without fear from you.
They stare at your fire,
Their darkness soaking in your light,
and shadows of the night reflecting off their starry pelts.

They wander in the sunshine, ever so freely,
Playing in the streams and rivers,
So much like our streets and avenues,
Leaping over the boulders and rocks,
Just as ancient to the land, just as intrinsic as we are,
Biting and licking each other,
Just as we love, we respect our kin.

The breeze carries them,
The alpha leads them,
and the human watches them.

Tails waving over the snow, over the ice, over the grass,
In the fresh air, in the stale.
Ears perking at every shriek, every human call,
Every mammalian bleat.
Tongues lolling as they streak left to right,

Dark coats blending into the deepness,
Light coats dissolving into the landscape.

Patterns of loudness and softness,
They run across the breadth of nature,
Beating their whiskers, sounding their howls,
and swishing their tails.
They sprint over and under, race across and through,
and pad all above.
We hear them every day, in every pattern, in every beat:
In the loudness of thunder,
In the softness of our heart,
and in the rumblings of the Earth.

THE CUB
BanWynn Oakshadow

BanWynn Oakshadow aka Suta Sunmanitu (Tough Coyote) is a hermit, hippie, experimental beat poet, speculative fiction writer, nature photographer, cultural historian, social activist, pipe carrier, husband, father, adult survivor of child abuse, mentally ill, gay, disabled veteran, and a Cancer with a criminal record. He uses every bit of that in his writing. This Jack-of-All-Trades/Master of None has no degrees in 8 interesting majors. He loves to create but hates the job of finding good homes for his work and is attempting to train his border collie to become his agent. BanWynn lives on a small, 400-year-old farm in southern Sweden in the middle of a remote forest grown over a Viking village gone a thousand years.

I hear the coming of him and pause. It is the fourth time that he has come so close to home. All that I have learned says to drive him off, or to run away. This is a dangerous animal; I've seen what they do to the deer in this forest. I do not run. I sit and watch.

A young male stumbles his way through the brush in my direction. It seems as if he must be intentionally shuffling through every drift of dry leaves. Maybe he is trying to catch each dry twig and break it off to let noise mark his passing. He looks to be barely more than a cub—gangly and gaunt; with paws still out of proportion to his body, and his muzzle far too short for his face. He looks, darting his head this way and that—hunting, if he dares call it that—but, he is unlikely to catch more than exercise for his efforts. Even as I watch, a rabbit startles behind him—only a few paces away—yet he does not so much as swivel an ear or turn to look. It escapes without his knowing that it was ever there. It seems the young of even this fearsome animal are born careless; needing to be taught.

Brush and ferns hide me well, the breeze is in my face, and so I sit and watch. Watch this rarely seen animal as he explores the area near where I am hidden. Though he looks often and knows even to look up as he hunts, he doesn't use his nose or, it seems, even his ears. He uses his too-large paws to push at a log. It takes several tries before the dead tree rolls over. Mice nest under that log, but they found retreat even as it shifted the slightest bit as he first pushed. Still he sits and digs in the wet earth beneath it. Maybe he will sate his hunger on the grubs there.

Instead, he closes a paw over one of the salamanders in the rot. They are not good for him to eat, but he will find that out for himself. It manages to wriggle free and disappear before his muzzle gets close. This reminds me that I have come here for a reason, but I resist. An opportunity to watch one of these curious, dangerous animals this close is too rare to pass up.

A call, high pitched and shrill, carries far—barely reaching through the leaves and needles of the forest. Following it, the harder to hear undulating call of what I know to be the alpha female of his small pack. He cocks his head and then stands. Using his hind paws, he rolls the log back into place and begins to lope to his den.

As he disappears from sight, I turn away from the strange, young animal that walks on two legs; sorry that this time I was not able to watch him remove his pelt. The foxitch under my legs and tail makes me wish that I could do the same. I continue my own hunt. Shaking out my gray fur, I turn to gnaw a burr from my tail. I inhale, taking in all that is around me, ears swiveling catch the sound of even the mouse scuttling under the leaves as it returns to its home under the log. The breeze lifts the white fur of my ruff, carrying the smell of my prey. The newly weaned cubs are hungry for something to chew on and play with as much as to eat. I follow the path of the rabbit that the young one scared off. My mate, my cubs, and my pack are waiting.

First Snow
BanWynn Oakshadow

Gently, the winds blowing,
and under shrouded moon,
graced fur shades to white.
Gathering shadows growing,
called as one by her boon,
sing praise into the night.
Pale orb, bless our calling.

White, the first snow falling.

Of one blood is the pack,
summoned by our mother,
one heart beneath pale moon.
Lone voice joins with brother,
in winter's breath numbing,
howls rising and fall croon.
Gray pack's song is calling.

White, her grace is falling.

Where orange flower blooms,
the red men are drumming,
cousins joining in song.
When the crescent moon looms,
welcome winter's coming,
brothers as one pray long.
Hear the first snow calling.

Spirits united in song,
The first snow is falling.

Requiem for Akela
Mark Onspaugh

Mark Onspaugh is a California native and the author of over fifty published short stories. Like many writers, he is perpetually curious, having studied psychology at UCLA, exotic animals at Moorpark College's EATM program, improv comedy with the Groundlings and special effects makeup with Thomas R. Burman, Rick Baker and Rob Bottin. Mark has also written for film and television. His first novel The Faceless One *is available on Amazon from Penguin Random House's Hydra imprint. The sequel to* The Faceless One, Deadlight Jack, *was published by Penguin Random House in January of this year. Cemetery Dance has just published* The Forsaken, *an anthology he co-edited with author Joe McKinney. His kaiju novel* Kua'mau, Kaiju Moth of Wrath *and his zombie novel* The Thetis Plague *are available on Amazon from Severed Press. He currently lives in Morro Bay, California with his wife, writer Tobey Crockett and two tricksters who have taken the form of cats. You can visit him at www.markonspaugh.com*

San Diego, 2075.

The last gray wolf slept fitfully in a cage of concrete and iron. He lay on a bed of straw, a basin of water and a bowl of watered-down Purina Wolf Chow close by. Off in the corner lay a well-chewed rubber bone, discarded and forgotten because one of his primary canines was broken, and his gums were sore.

His name was Akela, and he had been named for the alpha of Mowgli's wolf pack in *The Jungle Book* by Rudyard Kipling. Once he had been strong and swift, now he was gaunt and his muzzle had gone nearly white. His old bones were plagued by arthritis, and he did little except sleep.

Akela sighed, his wolf dreams of running through dark and verdant woods with his pack offering a marked contrast to his reality.

As the last gray wolf, he was housed in the "Vanishing Species" section.

The zoo was quiet, and even many of the nocturnal species were asleep. There were no patrolling night watchmen—

security duties fell to automated drones who sent a video feed to the security office in the administration building.

A faint click of fine leather shoes sounded on one of the pathways a quarter mile to the north.

Akela, whose hearing and sense of smell were still good, pricked up his ears in his sleep.

After a moment a man appeared, dressed in expensive but casual clothes. Had he wanted to, he could have approached in total silence, but he had made some sound as a courtesy to the old wolf, the object of his late night visitation.

To call the visitor a man was something of a misnomer. He had been a man once, but those days were many centuries behind him. Still, we will continue to call him a man for expedience if not accuracy.

The visitor was tall and pale, with stern and regal features. His hair was lustrous and jet black, and swept back over his skull. His brows, thick and bristling, arched over eyes so black they seemed not to have any white whatsoever.

The man came to a stop before Akela's cage, his nose wrinkling at the scent within. His sense of smell was comparable to the wolf's, but even if it were not, he would still be able to tell the cage had not been cleaned in several days.

His eyes flashed with anger at the negligence, the lack of respect.

Calming himself, the man knelt and reached through the bars. A sound came from his throat, something between a growl and a whimper.

Akela opened his eyes. He roused himself and moved on shaky legs toward the outstretched hand. Because of his pain and discomfort, he might have bitten any other hand. But he sniffed the proffered hand and then licked it.

The man dissolved into a white mist that moved with deliberation through the bars.

Once past the bars, he became a man again.

The man knelt by the wolf and Akela whimpered, sounding for the first time in years like a exuberant pup. His tail wagged like a joyful metronome, something his keepers would have thought impossible.

It pained the man that this noble creature was locked up, a prisoner to humanity's arrogance and ignorance. A militant group known as the Natural Selectionists had sought to ban any extraordinary means to save a species. They felt extinction was a noble and natural process.

And so here he was, the first of his kind with the last of *Canis lupus.*

They sat together for nearly an hour, then the man stared into Akela's eyes.

The old wolf collapsed with a sigh—not dead but deeply asleep.

The man went to the door. The lock was a primitive mechanism, and he was able to pick it easily.

He hoisted the unconscious wolf up over his shoulder and left the cage. He had noted that the Vanishing Species section was far larger than the last time he had visited, and he resolved to do something about that.

They were not detected by the drones. His form had thwarted mirrors and cameras for millennia—why should a flying camera be any different? Akela's proximity rendered his form amorphous and pixilated, something dismissed as a glitch by the attendant in the security office.

The disappearance of the last wolf from a locked cage warranted no more than a curiosity piece in the various news feeds. The public was far more interested in a murder case where a famous celebrity had found his ex in a compromising position with his clone. Truth be told, most people were content to visit virtual environments where the animals were more approachable, and—in some programs—could even talk and become boon companions.

Of greater concern was the theft of various specimens of frozen animal ova and DNA. But now most of the government's research money was being spent on defense or the terraforming of Mars. No one outside of the scientists and a few old timers cared much about the DNA or gametes of obsolete species.

Carpathian Mountains, 2080.

High on a parapet of his ancestral home, the man looked out over the acres of forest he had reestablished. It had taken several hundred years to recreate the primeval forests of his youth, utilizing research he had funded to develop stronger strains of trees and undergrowth. That same technology had also been employed on Mars.

Those who still knew the old stories about him might be surprised to know he had vast real estate holdings, both here and on the Red Planet. Soon those species he had rescued from extinction would fill the forests, jungles and deserts of Mars—making it truly like Eden.

Oh, he knew that humans would soon grow tired of the glittering jewel Mars would become, and they would begin to rob, rape and pollute it, just as they had *their* ancestral home.

He would be ready—he and his kind had always been the guardians of the wild.

But that was a matter for another time. For now, he listened to the children of Akela as they ran through the forest, singing to the moon in joyous and riotous abandon. The forest resounded with their ancient and poignant song.

The Children of the Night.

What music they make!

THE GUARDIANS
MARTA ANNA PODOLSKA

Marta Anna Podolska is a self - taught artist and book illustrator from Poland, who has been living all around Europe, with the U.K. being currently her home. She has been drawing from the very moment she first grabbed a pencil, her biggest inspiration are animals and Disney animated feature films. Wolves are her favorite animals and she strongly identifies her personality with those magnificent canines. Apart from drawing she also loves painting with watercolors, reading books, writing stories, traveling and learning languages.

I am of Wolf
Marta Ann Podolska

MINE
MARTA ANN PODOLSKA

ATTENTION ALL
ANNA DU PUGET

It was thanks to her mother, who was a talented artist herself, that Anna Du Puget was encouraged to pursue her own artistic talent, and she went on to complete a Foundation Course at Maidenhead College of Art after leaving School. Then going on to do Graphic Design at Goldsmiths, University of London, but she soon realized that her interests lay with photography. Always out taking photos and reporting on events in London in the 70's, it was no wonder that she eventually went on to study photography at the Berkshire College of Art and Design.

Her first job as a professional photographer was working in scientific photography and then later as a medical photographer at the local hospital, photographing traumas and many horrific injuries and diseases that needed to be photographed for journals, as well as for record purposes. She found this quite a hard experience.

But having a great love of the countryside and animals eventually led her to work as a freelance, photographing at dog shows and various events. She has always had a special place in her heart for wolves and has been fortunate to be able to photograph them up close and even stroke one at a wolf sanctuary.

Her studio work involved working with people and children and she is an experienced animal photographer, illustrator and writer. She is friendly and approachable, and her webpage is www.annadupuget.co.uk

HOWLING WOLF
ANNA DU PUGET

I Can See right Into Your Mind
Anna Du Puget

A Time for Wolves
Hemal Rana

Born and raised in North Jersey, Hemal Rana is an avid reader and writer. His love for wolves began at a young age and continues to grow to this day. This is his third published work for Thurston Howl Publications, but it won't be his last. With this new piece, Hemal continues to build up his resume and hopes to one day add a full-length novel to his bibliography. The dream continues.

Wolves love the winter season
It's as simple as that
In the winter, they are in their element
Just as the night is the element of the bat

Other species however don't like the winter
They see it as a time of darkness and death
Humans especially dislike the winter season
To them, the winter is as dark as the story of Macbeth

In their literature, they illustrate their dissatisfaction with
winter
Winter is when the world around us disappears from sight
A period when darkness grows and the cold surrounds us
Where people pray for a sign of the summer light

Wolves however have a different point-of-view
They enjoy the cold and the occasional frosty breeze
They love the colorful leaves that signal the coming of
winter
They would prefer if Jack Frost decided not to leave

It's not surprising that wolves are seen as the beasts of
darkness
The literary symbols of everything unholy and eternal woe
But the wolves don't care about how the humans depict
them
Just as long as they can enjoy the snow

THE WOLF CALLED GRANT
ANN ROBERTS

After a life-changing stint in journalism, Ann Roberts' main interest in writing has manifested to focus on non-fiction essays, poetry, and short stories. Roberts has a deep appreciation for the art of creative writing and aspires to always improve her abilities as a writer.

Stan had always been somewhat indifferent about animals. His father was allergic to fur, and his mother had a strong aversion to bacteria of any kind. Having a pet would destroy the perfectly disinfected quarantine of their one-story ranch house in the middle of the burbs. When one of their neighbors' cats leapt up on their kitchen windowsill on fish night, during Stan's childhood, his mother almost had a full-blown panic attack. Stan had little to no experience with animals of any kind. Birds pooped, cats scratched, dogs barked. Those were mere facts he had observed from a distance.

Now Stan was living on his own in an apartment, working full-time at Rizzo's Italian Bistro. He had taken the past year off from college, and was trying to start saving money while figuring out what he wanted out of life.

"Hey, there buddy," Stan said warmly, setting down the takeout box with odd scraps of chicken parmesan and meatball sub mixed together with other random dishes from that day. He felt better about feeding a hungry stray than throwing out the day's scraps for raccoons to scavenge later.

Grant always came around 11 p.m., right when Stan closed Rizzo's Italian Bistro for the night. Stan would lock down the front of the building and take the garbage out to the dumpster in the back alley. For the past three months, Grant had waited for him. Stan did not particularly mind. It was nice to have the company.

Grant ate gratefully.

"Had a good day there, Grant?" Stan asked, yawning.

"Yeah, mine was alright too."

Stan picked the name Grant to call him, since the dog had no collar. Stan had always liked the name, and Grant seemed to Stan to be a noble and placid creature, deserving of it. A husky or a German shepherd, Stan assumed, without knowing how to tell the difference.

Stan waited for the large dog to finish eating then disposed of the Styrofoam container.

"Good boy," he said, closing the trashcan lid.

Stan never pet the dog. His parents had never shown him how. These nightly visits from Grant were Stan's closest experience to having a pet.

"Well, buddy, I hope you have a good night and find somewhere nice to sleep," Stan said, starting the three-block walk to his apartment.

Stan's mother always warned her son to never feed strays. "They won't leave you alone!" But with Grant, Stan felt a mutual understanding. He was just there for the food. Grant did not expect any more. It worked out.

That night Grant followed him out of the alley and across the street by the park, and then sat to watch his human disappear around a corner.

That was their relationship. Stan gave him food, and Grant did not bother him any more than that.

One day during the late lunch hour, Grant came back to Rizzo's Bistro. It was the first time he had appeared there in the daylight, and his thick coat shimmered in the sunlight. He sat outside of the black metal fence around the outdoor seating area. Stan finished taking a couple's order and serving them drinks when he caught a glimpse of his nightly beggar out of the corner of his eye.

"Why hey there, buddy," he greeted him with slight concern. "What's the matter, Grant? You're here really early.

You ok?"

Grant's tranquil eyes stared back at Stan but betrayed no message, no vulnerability.

Confused, Stan retreated back to the restaurant to place the customer orders. Grant remained.

"Hey guys," he said to the hostess and cook. "That beggar dog I've been telling you about is here."

Kim, a snippy young hostess, handed Stan a small basket of bread to take out to his patrons on the patio. She peeked out the open front door at the homeless dog on the curb.

"Stan, I think that's a wolf," Kim said without so much as a second take.

"A wolf? How can you tell?" Stan asked.

"It just doesn't look like a normal husky to me, I grew up with huskies."

Their conversation sparked the curiosity of Bob, one of the cooks, and he popped out from behind the kitchen counter to look over at the so called wolf.

"What would a wolf be doing all the way out here? I don't think there is anywhere nearby he could've come from besides the downtown zoo," he said.

"I don't know. Think we should we call animal control?" Kim responded.

Stan didn't hesitate. "No."

They looked at him quizzically.

"Sorry," he said. "I don't feel like we need to. He's not hurting anybody. I'm pretty sure he's not rabid. He's just our chilled out neighborhood watchdog."

"Wolf," Kim corrected.

"Watch-wolf doesn't sound right. Anyways, it doesn't matter because Grant is fine. He's not bothering anybody. See? The customers aren't batting an eye. They think he's just somebody's dog. Which he kind of is," Stan said defensively.

"Are you claiming ownership now?" Kim challenged.

"No," he said. "But I do kind of feel responsible for him. He's been eating our scraps, you know."

"Look, just get it away from the customers. It's bad for business if there's a flea-infested wild animal on our doorstep," she hissed under her breath so that the customers by the window couldn't hear her. "And get that bread out there," she said, noticing the basket still in his hands.

Stan heeded Kim's warnings, and the transaction with Grant had been simple. Stan looked him over to see if he had come to nurse a recent injury, but saw nothing of note. He tossed him two burnt meatballs he had slipped in his apron pocket, and firmly asked Grant to leave. Grant did. The problem was solved.

However, three days and nights passed after that, and Grant did not come back. Stan grew worried and wondered if he had said anything to upset the calm, cool, and collected creature he fed every night. Fretting over the absent beggar, Stan sat at table four shredding a paper napkin when he should have been sweeping. He asked Kim and Bob if he had been too harsh with the creature.

"It's not a person," Kim reminded him, impatient with his fretting. "It doesn't understand human language."

"You don't get it. Grant was really smart," Stan said gloomily. "He knows what I'm talking about. I just don't know where he is."

"Could have gotten hit by a car," Bob suggested.

Kim glared at him.

"That's what I'm afraid of," Stan said quietly.

Almost a week after Stan sent Grant away, a shoeless and sloppily clad man arrived in front of Rizzo's during the late lunch lurch. He stood outside, looking into the building.

Kim saw him first.

"Stan, go tell that guy where the homeless shelter is."

The man seemed to relax when he saw Stan approaching. "You're here," the man said in a dry voice.

"Yes sir, may I help you with something?" Stan asked professionally, trying to draw the man away from the Rizzo's entrance.

"You know me," the man said, his eyes betrayed a hopeful desperation.

Stan was startled.

"I'm sorry, sir, I don't."

"Grant," the man said gravely.

Stan's neurological functioning began overheating. He started thinking about his lost watchdog-wolf.

"What? What are you saying, sir?"

"I am Grant," the man said earnestly.

That serene furry face came to Stan's mind and regret tightened around his heart.

"Your name is Grant, sir?" he tried to recover under a web of confusion. "Very nice to meet you. My name is Stan, as you can see from my name tag -"

The man looked at Stan's indicated nametag with disinterest. "Ah."

"Are you planning on dining with us today, mister Grant?"

"Mister?" the man thought about the word.

"The soup special is -"

"You ok, buddy?" the man interrupted, his eyes piercing through Stan's. Those deep, knowing eyes.

Stan's mind went back to feeding that quiet and respectful animal. The words and phrases the man who called himself Grant said all reminded Stan of things he had said to the stray dog he named Grant.

"I don't get it," said Stan, talking to the man called Grant. "Are you like some sort of reverse werewolf? What would that be even? A wolf-human? That doesn't make sense." Stan asked as he took his usual break in the back alley with Grant.

The man called Grant did not have any answers himself. All that he knew was that he had been a wolf, and a human called Stan used to feed him in the back alley of Rizzo's. His wolf self had started to feel strange the day he came in during the late lunch hour. After a couple of days he could not remember. The wolf named Grant woke up with the body of a human. A couple of homeless people discovered him in the park in a state of nature and offered him some tattered clothing they could live without, seeing his need was greater.

The man called Grant went to the only human he thought he could trust, his faithful feeder.

He also found that he could communicate a limited amount in Stan's human language, repeating phrases he had heard and piecing together statements from his new human mouth's vocabulary.

"But I don't know what to do or how to help you," Stan said. "I don't know if I even believe that you are my wolf, Grant. You could just be some weird guy who noticed the other day that I sent him away," Stan's mental list of possible scenarios expanded.

"I am Grant," the man said again, uninterested in explaining anything else and unable to in the first place.

"This is crazy," Stan repeated to himself under his breath as he took the excess throw pillows off his navy blue denim couch.

Stan looked at his guest. The man called Grant stood turning his head all about him, visually soaking in what his human friend considered a decent living space. As quiet and respectful as ever, he stayed where he was and waited patiently for further instruction or invitation.

Stan stood up, flustered. The couch cushions were now tightly covered with a pristine fitted sheet.

"I cannot believe I am letting a strange homeless man sleep on my living room couch just because he says he's the human version of the dog I feed –"

"I am a wolf," the man called Grant corrected graciously. "You are not working?" he had only seen Stan in the context of the bistro.

"I asked for an early night off," Stan said. He looked at the clock, "I'm going to bed."

"Good night," the man called Grant said, still standing where he was when he first entered the apartment.

The man called Grant stood in the middle of Stan's apartment as his host slept off his confusion; the man-wolf uncomfortably looked at the cramped space, longing for the open sky. He had never been indoors before. His home was under the stars. The night was his realm. He had gotten lost in the city over three months ago and claimed the slightly wooded public park as his safe harbor. The four walls of his human friend's dwelling were too small. The window held only a view of the tall building beside them. There was no life here.

Remembering how Stan used the doorknob earlier, Grant turned it and walked out to the hallway. He went down the stairs all the way to the street; the door was propped open for a first floor smoker's convenience. The air smelled fresher there. He stayed out for hours. Finding the place in the park where he usually slept, he tried getting comfortable there again, but his new body would not allow it. He could not sleep there as he once did. He tried running on his human legs through the trees in the park as he often did, but now his naked feet felt every rough or sharp object on the ground, and the trees ran out within a minute or two of the jaunt. Scared and unhappy, he went back to Stan's apartment. The couch prepared for him was strangely comfortable, and he slept for the remaining hours of the early morning.

Exhausted, Stan wandered through his apartment the next morning in search of his coffee maker. He had only a vague recollection of what happened the night previously. With mug in hand, he went about his daily routine, looking about in confusion when he did not feel the throw pillows at his back on the couch as he usually did. Then he saw the tattered clothes lying over the now dirty fitted sheet on which he sat.

He caught a glimpse out of the corner of his eye. Whipping his head around, he let out a scream for three reasons. Firstly, because the swift movement in his still stiff body caused a muscle spasm in his neck. Secondly, because he was so surprised to see the wolf called Grant sitting dutifully beside the couch, and then remembering the odd day he had yesterday. And thirdly, in his surprise and sudden muscle pain, Stan dropped his mug and spilled coffee all over himself.

But he was a human last night wasn't he? Everything scrambled in his mind. He took off his soaked shirt and tried mopping up the couch but eventually settled on ripping off the soiled fitted sheet while he talked to Grant.

"How are you a dog – wolf again? Why are you here?"

The wolf sat where he was and bowed his head.

"No, I didn't mean it like that," Stan began, tossing the wad of wet cloth on the floor beside his bedroom door.

Later, they sat listening to the crickets in the dark, the distant sounds of cars driving along the perimeter of the park and the occasional dog bark. Grant sat by the bench like a dutiful watch-wolf at attention. Stan reached over to pat his head for the first time. Grant was good. He did not complain or make a mess, besides the dirty fitted sheet. There was an overwhelming sense of serenity that came over Stan when Grant was there. Just petting the creature and scratching him behind his ears was a therapeutic exercise. He had never imagined that owning a pet would feel so relational, but he did not own Grant. Grant was a wolf. People did not own wolves. Grant would not be happy living with Stan. Would he? He seemed so lost. Not necessarily needy, but unsure of his place, much like Stan himself.

The old black and white Wolf Man movie Stan remembered seeing as a kid was so dramatic and violent. The man who turned into a wolf lost control, went crazy, ate a bunch of villagers. But Grant was a wolf who turned into a man. He was already self-contained to start with. The transition from species did not, to Stan, seem to dramatically alter his stoic exterior, so what was the point of it?

"I wish you could tell me how to help you, buddy," Stan said sadly.

The two sat in the park for a while and soaked in the slightly nippy night.

For the first time for quite a while, Stan had asked for the entire day off. That morning Stan had discovered the wolf had become the man again overnight. They spent the morning talking and getting nowhere. But one thing was certain: Grant needed to find where he had come from before he was lost in the city three months ago. They were going for a drive.

The more he talked to Grant, Stan realized he had lived by himself with a stilted disconnection from other people and animals. His parents did not really help him develop that. Helping Grant was an odd sensation that gave Stan a sense of fulfillment he hadn't had previously.

As Stan drove Grant home, he thought about his relationships with others. He tried to keep in touch with his folks, but often forgot to check in with them. He did not really have friends over much, or at all. His coworkers were just that. He had not been on a date for years. He looked over at the man-wolf in his passenger seat. This was the most time he had spent with someone in a long time.

What Stan felt as he watched Grant inspect the opening of the deep forest outside the city limits was both hope for his wolfy friend and regret that they could not stay together.

"Does this seem familiar to you?" Stan asked.

"I'm not sure," Grant said, sniffing the air. He would have been a wolf last time he was here, so his assessment using his human senses was skewed.

Suddenly there came a howl from the nearby trees. Stan jumped. Three wolves that looked similar to Grant's coloring and size appeared and stared at the odd pair of humans. For a moment, Stan was afraid of being eaten.

"Do you recognize them, Grant?" Stan asked, but the man beside him was gone.

The wolf called Grant looked up at him. Grant and Stan's eyes locked and a silent understanding set between them.

"Good job, buddy," Stan said. "Take care of yourself."

The wolf called Grant gave a slight nod. Stan reached down to pat his head one last time. Then he watched Grant go over to the other wolves in the forest, and they sniffed about him and murmured. From what Stan could tell, it was all welcoming greetings.

There was something special about Grant, Stan mused. *Perhaps his extensive separation from his own kind had triggered a supernatural man-wolf curse.* Whatever it was, Grant was home.

Stan returned to his little 2-room apartment and stood looking at the space. It was small. Barely enough room for him. He tidied the pillows on the couch where a wolf turned into a man and vice versa. Stan wondered how Grant was, back with the other wolves. He wondered if he would be alright.

Stan looked at the clock. He'd need to get up early for work in the morning. The routine was back. The pre-Grant routine. Work all day, then home to bed and repeat. He looked at the dirty wad of sheets still on the floor from the other day. It was real. It happened. There was a manwolf at Rizzo's, but now he was gone.

Stan did not feel tired and in a spur of impatience, he left his apartment. The night was quiet. He went back to the park, passing the spot where he had sat on the bench talking to his wolf friend. He kept walking. He felt odd, and he wanted his friend back. Was Grant his only friend? Did he really have nobody else to talk to?

He wondered how strange it would be to change into a wolf out in the park, mirroring the transformation Grant had undergone.

Stan decided he was not done with Grant yet. Pausing, he pulled out his cell phone and dialed a number. His mother picked up.

"Mom," Stan said. "How's it going? Is it too late?"

"Oh no, dear, we were just reading," she answered in a cheerful voice. "Bill, it's Stanley," she said to her husband. "Oh, honey, tell me, what's been going on with you these days? It's been so long. How's work? Have you made any new friends?"

Hearing her excitement at his call and both of his parents murmuring old couple things to each other as they fumbled with activating speaker-phone, Stan smiled.

"Well, sonny," his father said as they finally switched on the speaker. "What have you got to say for yourself?"

That was a regular fatherly greeting that used to annoy Stan, but now it made him feel less alone. Stan felt relaxed talking to them after so long.

"Well, guys," Stan said warmly to his parents. "I made a new friend. His name's Grant."

"Oh wonderful, darling!"

"That's great, son."

"Tell us all about him! Is he from the bistro?"

"Yeah, he was a regular for the past few months, but he just moved back closer to his family a little ways out of town."

"Well, I hope you keep in touch with him," his mother said.

"I think I will mom," Stan said. "He's a really neat person."

UNITY
VIRGINIA MARIA ROMERO

Virginia Maria Romero is a visionary artist with works in public and museum permanent collections, as well as numerous private collections throughout the United States and abroad. Romero's biographical artist profile is included on the New Mexico Office of the State Historian website: www.newmexicohistory.org. In 2013 Romero was recognized as a distinguished Artist and Poet by the American Council for Polish Culture. "As an artist who is deeply concerned about protecting wildlife, I strive to make sure that my art helps to educate and motivate people to protect nature. A catalyst for meaningful change, the power of art lies in its ability to transcend and inspire and to guide us past established realities and prevailing ideologies."

WOLF
VIRGINIA MARIA ROMERO

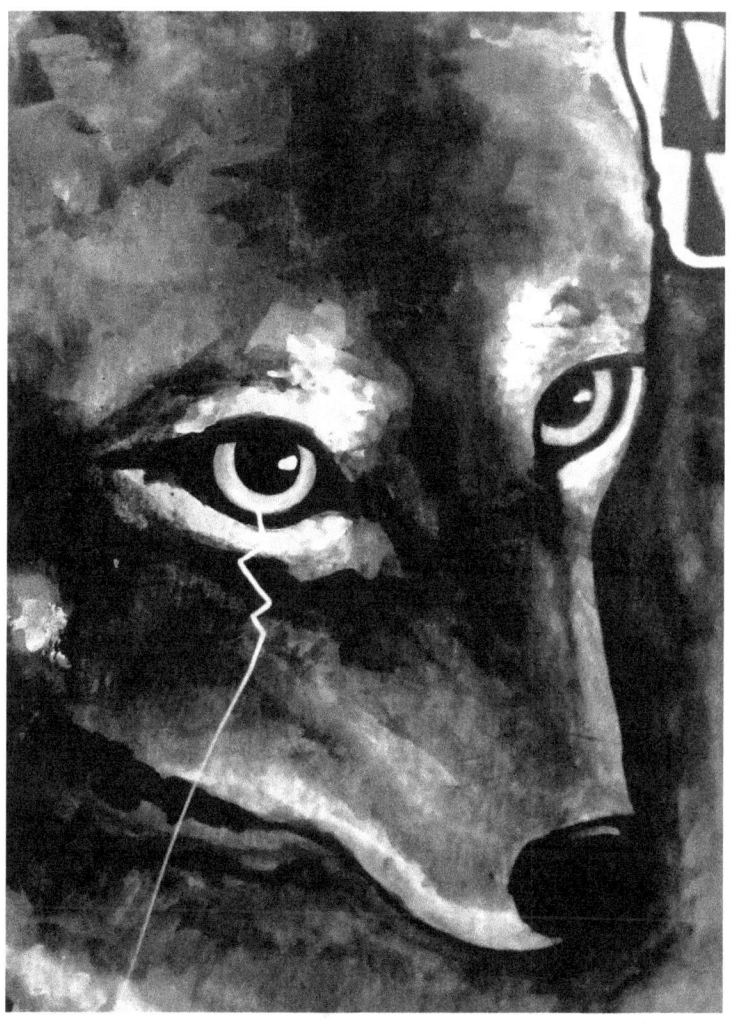

Yuna:Wikko'o
Virginia Maria Romero

Yuna:Wikko'o
Virginia Maria Romero

Wolf song,
a primal chorus that I dance to
as the fullness of my heart empties
into dreams that come with the sun's last breath
before buried beneath purple mountains.

These dreams
that tell me the wolf's song
will be kept alive
by our voices…

A primal song that fills my spirit

yuna:wikko'o
shiwi

Barely audible
yet piercing,
a primal call
Iktushiwi
Shalanitawu
Nakashawu
Yuna:Wikko'o….

The Divide of Light and Shadow
Bruno Schafer

Bruno Schafer is a writer and historian who lives in Indiana. He has been writing since he was fairly young and this passion for writing has stayed with him to this day. He writes a mish-mash of different genres that have varying themes and ideas behind them. His writing inspirations include Kenji Miyazawa, Richard Adams, and Kenneth Oppel. One of his publications was in the 3rd Wolf Warriors Anthology which contained the poem The Wolf's Song *which was published by Thurston Howl Publications.*

Zhi looked at the forest as she walked by the trees. Buds bursting forth as she passed. The flowers blossomed as each paw tapped the ground with no more force than a feather drifting to the ground. Lifting her head to the sky, she closed her eyes and began to sing: "I am life, I am life. I bring the morning sun and the soft rain. I am the beginning of all. I am life."

The she-wolf's song danced across the air with the soft wind. With the song came the melting of the white snow that still dotted the ground, and in its place grew the green grass of early spring. And in the trees, singing along with her, were the birds who had returned from their winter homes in the south.

Following the conclusion of her song, she opened her eyes and looked at the blooming forest. A soft smile appeared on her face as she glanced at the flowering meadow in the distance, beyond the forest. However, amongst the colorful flowers was a single shape that seemed out of place, dark as the night sky and skulking through the grassy field. Zhi's face became brighter, though in that new brightness was a cold nervousness. She turned and began running down the path, hoping to reach the edge of the forest before the figure vanished.

Upon reaching the edge, Zhi gave a low howl to gain the

attention of the figure. "My shadow, I see you as you creep across the land" she sang. The howl had a rougher tone to it than her first song, though it maintained many of the same joyful notes.

The figure stopped and turned its lupine head toward Zhi. The darker wolf looked as thin as the branches on the trees. Its fur seemed like it had come from a starless night sky. However, the most striking feature was its piercing yellow eyes, eyes that seemed to give off a glow in contrast to the darkness of its fur.

The wolf's ears perked up, and it ran towards Zhi at a swift pace, as if trying to race the wind. The wolf seemed slightly unbalanced in its gait, but surefooted enough so that it wouldn't trip. Every step seemed calculated to prevent stepping on an uneven patch of ground.

"Zhi, it has been so long since we last talked." The wolf's voice was ragged and seemed to mix in with what remained of the cold winter wind. "I am glad to see you again."

"I am glad to see you too, brother Smer."

"How long has it been?" Smer kept his eyes from making even a moment's contact with his sister's, not out of any concern or respect but more out of wish to keep the peace. "I recall our last meeting ended with you chasing me off."

"Only because you went after a creature who still had life. You are only allowed to claim the dying."

"Sister, that is not for you to determine." Smer gave a small smirk, still keeping his eyes lowered. "But I understand. Just because of what I am, you think I am evil. No, dear sister, my job is my own. We don't exist in the extremes."

"How can you claim such a thing? Things are so vastly different for a reason."

"Yet we are not complete opposites. Many creatures consider me evil, but what about you?" Smer looked up at his sister. "You think of yourself as the ultimate good, and in many ways you are good, but what about those that are brought into life with no chance?"

"What do you mean?" Zhi demanded, "do you think I am an unfeeling monster?"

Smer sighed with exasperation. "No, I didn't mean that. In the end the light is no more good or evil than the shadows." Smer's eyes now reflected complete defiance. "Do you think anyone would be able to determine light without shadow? No, they must exist together, or not at all."

Zhi's ears fell at this. "How did you come to this conclusion, Smer?"

"Like you, many choose to avoid me, believing me to be evil or a portent of some negative force. Denying the purpose of my existence. Thus, I am left alone with my thoughts"

Zhi gave a sharp snarl at her brother's comment. "I do not seek to avoid you, or have you forgotten that I am the one who approached you?"

Smer gave a snort of laughter. "Yes, but you are afraid of me, your stance gives that away. Tell me, why are you scared, what would you have to fear? Damn it Zhi, answer me! Surely my own kin understands that they shouldn't fear me." Smer's tone became more aggravated with each passing word.

"I don't know, Smer. I don't know."

"Your children have suffered just as much as me, their uncle. Hunted as a threat, with so many of those hunting them seeming to ignore the clear and visible purpose that they serve. I have had to visit so many. Yet I can't express my sympathy to them. Can you possibly understand that?"

"Yes brother, I understand it perfectly. I have tried to help many of them as a mother should, but I am afraid I can't do that for all of them. I try and hope things will get better."

"After how long?" Smer asked, his eyes turning cold and sad, the eyes of one who has seen true sadness. "What guarantee do you have it won't be too late when it finally does?"

Zhi gave a harsh, shaking sigh. "I don't know, all I know is that things are changing. I hope for the better."

"Indeed." Smer turned toward the horizon. "I'd better leave. I am sure you don't want the spring to come late this year," he said, trying to lighten the mood.

Zhi gave a slight chuckle at her brother's joke. "Indeed," was all she said as her brother began to move away from the valley and to the south.

The last she saw of her brother was him standing against the southern horizon and giving a howl of farewell. "I am shadow, I am the dark. I bring the night's moon and the storms. I am the finishing cycle, I am not the end."

INVERT WOLF
DAWN SHARMAN

Dawn Sharman is a self-taught artist who lives in the UK with her husband Murray. She spends a lot of her time either sketching or writing and has almost completed a book, where one of the main characters is a wolf. She also likes to design and make jewelry, and has a keen interest in still life photography. She has a great passion for animals and nature and her designs have been used on many items including mugs and jigsaw puzzles. She also had two of her dog portraits exhibited in the Ideal Home Exhibition. Dawn gives up some of her time as a volunteer in a local charity shop, which raises money for a hospice.

OUT OF THE SHADOW AND INTO THE LIGHT
DAWN SHARMAN

The Old Wolf and the Light
Dawn Sharman

The old wolf lay sleeping in his den curled up upon the
ground,
keeping out the winter's chill that came from all around.
He had battle scars that he had acquired through the passing
years,
caused by facing his enemies and conquering his fears.
He had encountered hard times throughout his life along
the way,
dodging to escape bullets from the hunter's rifle,
if he hadn't, he would not have lived to be here today.

The years that followed taught him how to survive,
how to protect his own cubs so that they too could stay
alive.
He lay there sleeping, his eyes shut tight,
when suddenly he was awakened by a very bright light.
He opened his eyes and for a moment everything looked
blurred,
his body no longer ached of old age that he had endured.

He looked straight ahead of him with eyes opened wide,
and saw a large white wolf who beckoned him outside.
Once outside the white wolf spread out two large white
wings,
and soared into the night sky,
the old wolf suddenly found that he too had wings,
and that he also could fly.

It was a feeling of freedom and peace he had never
completely,
experienced before.

Higher and higher into the sky they both began to soar.
Until eventually amongst the stars they slowly faded away,
back at the den the old wolf looked peaceful where he lay.

DEN CAMERA
DANA SONNENSCHEIN

*Dana Sonnenschein is a professor at Southern Connecticut State University, where she teaches Shakespeare, folklore, and creative writing. Her publications include creative nonfiction and books of poetry (*Bear Country *and* Natural Forms*) as well as two chapbooks of prose poems. Individual works have appeared in journals such as* Epoch *and* Feminist Studies, *and are forthcoming in* Painted Bride Quarterly, Measure, *and elsewhere. She visits the Wolf Conservation Center regularly to sketch and paint, and has just completed the manuscript of a chapbook of poems focused primarily on the wolves who live there.*

Wolf Conservation Center, June 4, 2017

I spend Sunday night with a Mexican wolf and her ten-day-old pups. The rain is doubled, falling on trees outside my house and in, where la loba curls at the back of a corrugated pipe, a circle in a circle, as if I had the womb of the world on my laptop. Periodically, the three little ones wake and clamber over and under each other to find a teat, mewling and mumbling with effort. My cats believe the sound but aren't fooled by the image: the wolves aren't here. And yet they are, as the mother stretches and yawns, then folds back into her babies' world: one hind leg a land bridge they scale and burrow beneath, the curved slope of her belly, the ridges of forelegs, forehead, and nose. The pups push themselves into her body, nursing and wagging their tails. When they're done, she licks each one, even its bottom, so no scent can give away their presence to another predator.

At a sudden noise, she lifts her head, levers her body up, then trots purposefully past the camera, a wolf of light, there and gone. The pups huddle silently in the spot she's warmed. Moths flutter past. I'm almost meditating, sitting at some middle distance, aware of wings, rain on leaves and glass, and the cat who's just crawled onto my lap, her warmth, her fur, her purr.

Rustling. La loba has returned and turned, eyes glowing and otherworldly, a shadow who curls around darker forms to fall asleep. Until she rises slowly and lies down on her other side. Two pups immediately latch on, but a third curls against her head, nose between her ears, tiny body along her muzzle. A few moments later she lifts her face, eyes closed, and nudges him back inside her legs. I wonder if it's always the same pup, the one who rests with his chin on her hip, who climbs up only to tumble off her back, and if another insists on snuggling under her flank, and the third somehow always manages to take the warmest inside spot, belly to belly. Only she can tell these little wolves apart.

Their eyes will open soon, but for now they are in the dark. All three, black and gray. Enclosed in their mother's familiar scent, her fur layered with hints of blood, wet fern, and earth. La loba sighs in her half-sleep. As night dims the world outside, the pups squirm to curl around her neck, two with faces buried deep in her ruff, a third warming on her breath. Raindrops blur the window, and wind blows across the culvert, one long note and then another. I close my eyes, more there than here.

Armed With Hope...
Katarzyna Szopka

Originally from Poland, Katarzyna J Szopka is an inspiring young writer who has had a clear career path from a young age. The literary competition is her biggest hobby, which she hopes to change into a full-time job (or at least part-time) when she graduates from the University of Leicester (England) with a degree in Ancient History and Archaeology.

Since she was a young girl, she was full of ideas; she could create whole stories just by looking at a picture. When she started her education, she participated in many poetry competitions, and even won a few. One of the more recent ones was The Poetry Games – Midlands, *where she wrote poem called* Mother Suffering (Earth). *This poem was a chance for her to express the love she carries in her heart to the world.*

She hopes to do as much as she can to help those who are voiceless on their own. She was always fascinated by wolves and other wild animals because of their importance throughout history. She also understands the importance of conservation sites which help to ensure the continuation of such amazing creatures.

Just like poison kills the human body,
We are venomous to the heart of the Earth.

Burning and poisoning good,
Is in our nature...
Imprinted in our souls.

But they fight back
Daughters of the Luna,
Sons of the morning dew,
Armed in fog, and shiny fur.
Armed with hope
They fight back...

The sweet song of lost souls
Is what we hear in the forest.
They know that a wild heart

Can change their destiny
They call you my child!
They need your help!

To stand against your destruction,
To stand against your human greed!

To stand in line with Mother Nature.
To stand in line with the Kings and Queens of the forest.

BLACK WOLF WHITE BONE
ALLISON THAI

A Catholic Vietnamese-American hailing from Houston, Texas, Allison got her first taste of stories from true accounts of how her parents fled from communism as war refugees. Her imagination then grew like a weed from the likes of C.S. Lewis, J.R.R. Tolkien, Ursula Le Guin and Brian Jacques, while her love of wolves stemmed from Jack London and David Clement-Davies. When she's not studying for medical school, she hoards and devours secondary world/high fantasies, Russian historical fiction, Japanese comics, and biology in sci-fi. Her work earned Silver Honorable Mention in Writers of the Future and has appeared in Anak Sastra, Remixt, ROAR 8, Arcana - Tarot and Symbol of A Nation. She dug out a den for herself on Twitter as @ThaiSibir.

THE SAME WITHIN
ALLISON THAI

Katya and Kirill were fighting again.

No, not the sneaky jabs and light swats, the play fighting typical and healthy for cubs their age. Katya and Kirill bared tooth and claw at each other, with lips pulled back and eyes alight. They tumbled through the dirt, forming a flurry of black and white fur.

Masha had enough. "Katya, Kirill. Come here."

Her stern bark made them freeze, then they pulled off of each other. Kirill jumped back in time to avoid a swipe of Katya's paw, and they slunk toward Masha with ears lowered and their tails between their legs. The cubs came from the same litter, born a season too early as the harsh winter claimed the rest of their littermates. Save for a bent ear, Kirill looked as if he came away without a scratch, all thanks to his black fur. Dirt and tiny twigs, however, clearly matted Katya's white fur.

Their mother glared down at them. "Children, how many times have I told you not to fight among each other? You are blood, family—save your energy for the real fights of life and death."

The land man called Russia dealt a heavy blow on the wolves as well. Each day Masha and her pack roved and hunted to keep from starvation and laziness.

"She started it," Kirill muttered. "She thinks her fur's better than mine."

Katya turned up her nose. "Well, it's true. He looks like a crow, or a vulture, and he wouldn't be able to find anything in the winter."

"You'll stick out like a ghost at night," Kirill retorted. "Even the dumbest prey would spot you."

The cubs gazed wide-eyed up at their mother, imploring

agreement.

Masha gave neither of them the benefit of her choice; instead she shook her head and huffed a sigh. "Really, all this bickering over the color of your coats?" She'd reprimand them again and again, more times than she could count on her claws, and for all her authority as the *vysshiy* wolf, the cubs persisted in their petty quarrels. She decided on another approach. "Follow me."

Katya and Kirill exchanged confused glances before padding after her.

One of the *nizhniy*, Dmitri, raised his head. "You're taking them *there*?"

"We won't be long. Just look out for Roman and Vladimir. They should be back from their hunt soon."

Dmitri nodded, albeit reluctantly, and settled back on his scrawny haunches. He tried to act like a big brother to the two cubs, always looking out for them. Though in all honesty, Masha believed he only did a disservice to her youngest children. Dmitri worried too much and cried easily. He depended on the pack more than it depended on him. Surely he would die if left on his own—such as it was with most *nizhniy* wolves.

Kirill threw a worried glance back. "Will Dmitri be all right by himself?"

"It's just until your brothers return," Masha replied. "Dmitri can barely keep up in a hunt. He's best at guard duty." She meant that out of pity. If she'd been truly condescending she would have left him to fiercer wolves and bears many moons ago.

"That's what *you'll* be doing," Katya said to her brother. "You'd be a hopeless hunter."

"Same with you," Kirill hissed.

Masha whirled around with a snap of her teeth. "I don't want another word out of either of you." The cubs jumped back and yelped in fright. She jerked her head to the crags ahead. "Focus. We'll have to walk some ways to get where we need to be."

The cubs fell into a sullen silence, doing their best to keep up with their mother's long stride. Finally, Katya ventured a question: "Where are we going?"

"You'll see. We're almost there." Masha led them away from the plains and farther into the forest, where trees towered over them and only the oldest, largest roots poked through clumps of snow. Their legs not quite long enough, the cubs leapt and stumbled through the uneven terrain. Finally, they bumped right against their mother's legs when she halted.

"We're here."

Kirill's eyes were wide. "B-bodies everywhere. Wolf bodies."

Wolves did not practice burial. They believed in leaving their bodies out for the birds, so that their souls may be freed from their mortal cages to run and hunt among the rolling clouds. The cubs knew this custom, so Masha did not expect any questions regarding that.

"What happened?" Katya asked instead.

"A bear camealong and killed the entire pack." Masha closed her eyes and drew in a deep breath. "The snow covers its tracks, but I've lived long enough to know its stink when I smell it." Besides that, only bones remained to tell the grim tale. Much of the fur and flesh had been stripped away byever-greedy birds. Skulls grinned up at the cubs, who cowered behind their mother's flank.

"Do not look away," Masha murmured. "The dead remain dead. Would you rather they spring up and fight us for territory? There's nothing to be afraid of." She wanted her children to look at death square in the face, when their senses were not thrilled and filled by a feeding frenzy. There was no prey to savor and smell here, only the remains of their kind.

She wanted them to look long and hard, so that they may learn.

"Can you tell me who are the *vysshiy*?" she asked them. "The *sredniy*, or *nizhniy*?"

The cubs edged forward in tiny steps and craned their necks out, as much as their wavering courage could allow.

Katya frowned. "I...I can't tell."

"They're all just bones," Kirill said.

"That's right. Beneath the color of our coats we are all the same. We all bleed red. Our hearts beat the same rhythm. When we die, our bones turn yellow and white under the sun. The birds don't care what kind of rank their meal had carried in their past life."

The cubs shuddered, shaken by the weight of the truth their mother laid upon them.

Better to toughen them up early, Masha thought. Otherwise, they would meet the same cruel end as their father. Her mate did not survive his endeavor to provide food that winter. He left the birthing den, tried to hunt alone, and never returned. He never lived to see his newest litter. Masha did not even have time to find his body and mourn, for the pack had to move with haste to warmer lands or perish. She did not know where his bones rested now, only that the memory of him continued to rest and ache in her heart. Unlike most *vysshiy* who led their packs in pairs, Masha acted as both mother and father to her children. Roman and Vladimir, part of her first litter, were shaping up to be fine *sredniy*, mitigating the pack's routine functions of hunting, scouting, and looking after their younger siblings; soon they would grow to lead other *sredniy* and *nizhniy* wolves. Masha did not doubt that Katya and Kirill would follow in their brothers' pawsteps, if they learned.

"Until the time comes for you to find mates, leave me, and start your own packs, you must rely on each other to survive.

You can't live long in this world alone." Masha thought of her mate as she said this. "True, Katya may hide better in the snow with her white fur, and Kirill can blend in with the shadows because of his black fur. Use those advantages together, not against one another. Celebrate your differences. Don't pick on each other over them."

"We're sorry," Katya said.

Masha allowed a rare smile to cross her muzzle. "Don't apologize to *me*."

The cubs shuffled to face each other, then exchanged apologies to put their blows and insults in the past. Masha nodded in satisfaction. "Well, we're done here. Let's not keep the pack waiting."

At this their tails wagged and despite the long walk, they skipped eagerly alongside their mother. That night, for the first time since their birth, Katya and Kirill slept together. The cubs curled up against each other, black and white in harmony.

An Unforgettable Scene Beneath the Moonlight
Skyler Jon Thayer

With a Bachelor's Degree in English, Skyler Jon Thayer is a graduate from Stony Brook University. Although he misses the academic atmosphere, Skyler is enjoying life as he establishes himself as a writer. As a poet, Skyler has revived his old thoughts and memories that lived within him years ago. "An Unforgettable Scene Beneath the Moonlight" is a part of that manifestation. Furthermore, Skyler has given his hands a taste for various forms of writing: just recently, he began writing a column for the Great South Bay Magazine, *a local Long Island magazine.*

Under the night sky, she asked one question:
"Skyler, have you ever howled at the moon?"
As she gazed into the nightly heaven,
She quickly cried out an enthralling tune.
In return, I sang along with her howl.
From her small bosom, did mine eyes wander
Up towards her face— all fair, nothing foul.
Oh! Here can a heart only grow fonder!
Alas! That was the first and last we sung!
And although our time together was short,
I will never forget how her hair swung
Gracefully under Lady Luna's court.
Even with this sorrow and this heartache,
I always cherish her, never forsake.

LIGHT AND SHADOW WITHIN
FOREST WELLS

Forest Wells was first inspired by the events of 9/11. Though he didn't know anyone involved, the day lit his passion for writing, beginning with poems of emotion, transitioning to works of fiction. Wolves, and really all wild canines, are his second passion, which Forest put into his first published short story The Line, *as well as a longer young adult novel currently seeking publication. When he's not writing, you can find Forest cheering for the Los Angeles Chargers, the Arizona Coyotes, and either playing League of Legends, or watching the professional matches online. He also spends much of his free time volunteering with a local Girl Scout troop. Forest currently lives in his hometown of Thermal California. For more information about Forest Wells, check out his website at www.forestwells.com.*

It was the hardest day of my life.

My first hunt, my first journey with my father as an equal. It started so well.

It was I who found the trail, I who led us to the herd, I who pointed out the best target.

It was I who made the mistake.

We chased long and hard, driving the herd before us.

Each time it split, we stayed strong. He would feed our pack for days.

My younger brothers and sisters would grow strong on his flesh.

I felt the thrill, the chase, the expectation of the sacrifice given so we may live.

The joy spurred me further, separating our prey from his herd.

But I went too far alone. The group, small as they were, turned to face me.

I had left the pack behind. I faced three sets of antlers alone.

I had only myself to blame, and only myself to defend me.

My paws planted and pushed, frantic to escape.

Antlers chased me as I had chased them. Even my target came for me.

Stroke by stroke, my legs pushed to evade, but they were not enough.

A head ducked and pushed, sending sharp spikes into my flank.

Then it tossed, and I flew without wings into the trunk of a tree.

I hit the ground barely able to breathe.

My side bleeding, my head spinning, I tried to stand, but my legs would not move.

I heard the barks of my pack, some frantic, others excited.

They were continuing the hunt, as they should. One life is not worth more than the pack.

Still, some were coming for me, even though I knew it was too late.

My head spun faster, my breath came harder, and there was nothing for them to do.

My mistake, my hubris, and now, my end.

At last my eyes closed, and my body, pain and all, fell away.

I found myself in a land much like my own, yet brighter.

The sun, the trees, even the clouds seemed to glow as if all were on fire.

There was no pain, but no cold or warmth either.

It just was, as if the land were an extension of my own body.

The air was the only thing to be cool, though even it seemed to fill me with something more than breath. Were I not already dead, I would think I were breathing life itself.

I lifted my nose in search of others. I found but one scent.

I followed it through a meadow as soft as my fur, to a river running gentle like my mother's tongue. There on the banks, sat a figure.

A wolf of fur so purest white it seemed as if he could roll

in mud and remain clean.

I approached, ears and tail low. Respect for territory not my own.

The wolf turned to me, ears forward, but no rise in his fur or tail.

"No need for that," he said. "You are safe and welcome here."

His voice was even and sure, as if his words were his will unchallenged.

Yet his aura, the feeling I got from him, put me at ease like nothing I had felt before.

"Who are you?" I asked.

"I am the Wolf of light.

I am the joy of family, the thrill of the hunt, the free sense of running, the close bonds of the pack. I am boundless play and eternal bliss. I am a full stomach, a gathering howl, the fur of loved ones, and honored alpha.

I wait for you in the days after you can no longer hunt."

"Is that not today?" I asked.

He gave no answer. He only looked to the woods.

There I saw another figure, another wolf.

She approached with steps hard and heavy, as if she carried two members on her back.

Her fur was a black deep enough to absorb any light that touched it.

As she sat beside the other, all light fell into her, yet still surrounded her like a veil not quite there. Her body bore scars of battles won, and hunts well earned.

"I greet you," she said.

Her voice was soft and soothing, much like my mother's when I was young.

There was no pain in her tone, even as I saw her tail was missing its tip.

"Who are you?" I asked, hoping to sound curious with

respect.

"I am the Wolf of Shadow,
I am the turmoil of the pack, the pains and fear of wounds
and famine. I am the daily struggle, the strife all wolves must
overcome. I am the warrior, pack defender, there for the kill
of prey and rival, and I am the silent hunter, in search of
the next sacrifice.
I stand with you as you find your way in life."
My mind turned in every direction at once.
"I don't understand," I said. "Who are you? Why am I
here?"
"We are you," the light wolf said. "We are in you in every
step of your journey."
"We are them," the shadow wolf said. "We are in the pack
you care for."
Then they spoke as one, their voices clear and merging into
a single tone.
"We are all wolves."
Though I would not call it complete, understanding formed.
These two, whoever they may be, were the spirits of all
wolves.
Two sides of our being to carry us through our lives.
Hearing their voices, seeing their fur, feeling their aura,
I began to understand how each wolf fed on different
portions of them both.
Light and shadow affecting their lives and personality.
As I wondered where I sat on that balance, I remembered a
question left unanswered.
"Why am I here? Is this what comes after death?"
"No," the light wolf said. "This is a crossing. This is where
we wait to greet those that are to pass on."
"Your time is not yet come," the shadow wolf said. "You
still have much to journey toward."
"Then why am I here?" I asked.

"To learn of us," the light said. "The world needs us now more than ever."

The shadow said, "By taking us with you, by infusing us into your blood, you may yet share it with your kind, and with many other kinds."

"How can I share it with other kinds when I cannot speak with them?"

They spoke together once more.

"Carry us in your eyes. When others see us there, they will know of us, and become greater than they were before."

Then the shadow spoke alone. "Now go young one. Return to your pack."

The light said, "We will meet again, when your journey has ended."

Before I could form another thought, the land faded from view.

All was black and empty, and I reached out to try and remain.

I wanted to learn more of them. To understand them better.

Alas, I returned to my place under the tree.

My head ached, my side stung from my wounds, I was in pain, but alive.

Beside me lay my father.

He was caring for my wounds, staying with me as thought returned.

I tried to stand, but my father stopped me.

"Be at ease my son," he said. "Let your body recover before you stress it."

I rolled onto my belly so I could at least lay more comfortably.

As my head cleared, I turned to check my wounds.

Even without my father's care, I saw they were only shallow punctures.

They would hurt for a time, but not for long.

However, memory returned, dragging my ears down in shame.

"I'm sorry father," I said. "I was a fool."

He only laughed.

"So was I on my first hunt. Your lesson came easier than mine. I…"

He stopped when his eyes met with mine.

We stared into each other, and I could feel my soul touching his.

I could feel them, splitting from me to enter him.

Both wolves, both halves of us, were becoming clear to him for the first time.

"Did something happen to you?" he asked at last.

Now it was my turn to laugh. I had no other reaction to what I'd seen.

"Yes father. I… we, have something to share with the pack."

The Interim
April Young

April Young holds a PhD from the University of Arkansas and is an Associate Professor of English, and her works have been published in both creative and scholarly journals. She spends her time reading, writing, and caring for the myriad creatures who visit her farm.

When Maisy got sick, I skipped class and drove the two hours home from college, my mind spinning with the revolution of the wheels beneath me. Maisy had seemed tired when I'd last visited, but I'd assumed it was nothing—or at least not that. Her sleep schedule, like mine, had always been erratic, and she'd taken in new fosters: two young boys who pulsed with energy and never let her rest. I'd had no idea her listlessness was symptomatic of her condition, and my guilt nearly suffocated me.

By the time I got to her, Maisy could barely stand, her eyes rolling back and spittle coating her chin. Her tongue was swollen so that speech was impossible, but I understood her demand when she placed her narrow hand on my shoulder. She wanted Mammy—and so did I.

The sun was gone when we reached Mammy's mountain, but the woods are never dark. I took the incline as though I drove it every day, as though it hadn't been ten years since I'd roamed Mammy's woods and tumbled through the fields. Each mile that closed the distance between my grandmother and me cleared the fog from my mind and brought back her electric scent in waves so that, even as I carried a half-dead woman to her door, I could barely suppress my joy.

The candle burning on the porch made Mammy's gnarled frame almost straight again, the way it must have been before I was born, and the wind whipped her thick gray plait over her shoulder and down to her knees. Unlike her shadow, Mammy was motionless, a rigid series of angles and a show of white between her lips.

She lifted Maisy from my arms without difficulty, pressing her nose into Maisy's forehead and crooning a wordless song. The effect on my guardian was immediate; Maisy's breath evened and the lines of pain slid from her face. I, too, felt the tension slip from between my shoulders.

I followed Mammy into the house, down a narrow hall, through a cavernous den, and back into the night. The air seemed cooler there: wet, caught and shielded by the advancing forest, and threaded with dew. When Mammy placed Maisy on the ground atop a fraying quilt, the undergrowth seemed to sigh, music that made the leaves dance on the branches above.

Time may have slowed; it may have quickened. I could not tell. Just when I despaired of finding it, the noise of the procession beyond the trees came to my ears, a near-silence that rang with a quick intake of breath, a rapid beat of a heart. The only thing stronger than the sound was the scent, burning my nostrils and settling on my tongue.

Maisy found strength enough to turn her head to the woods, to search for the steadily winking flames, some green, most yellow, an occasional pair of red, gazing back at her. She stretched her arm to the edge of the quilt, palm open, fingers curled. A low hum, collective and satisfied, raised the flesh on my arms.

Despite my fear, I took a step forward. Mammy stayed me with a hand against my chest and a snarl that sent me back into the house.

The scent was subtler inside, but strong enough to lull me into a contented haze. I marveled at the pervasive peace of Mammy's mountain and wondered how I'd forgotten such serenity during the long years away, and then I slept.

As always, I dreamed of my mother, the half-formed image of a beautiful woman turning out of the light and joining a shadowed throng, Mammy holding my arm in spite of my cries. This time, however, Mammy released me; I could go if I wanted. The idea thrilled me at first—but the bereavement in Mammy's eyes, the thought of her alone and waiting, kept me back. Even in sleep I was bound to the law.

The pressure of Mammy's hands on my scalp and her fingers in my hair was comforting if not painless, and I nested my head in her lap, trying to return to sleep. She let me rest there for a moment before pushing me away. I blinked against the first light of morning, stretching the stiffness out of my legs.

Mammy waited until I was fully alert to answer my unspoken question with a nod of her head: Maisy had gone in the night.

"I don't understand," I told her, shaking my tangled head. "She's not that much older than me. Why would they want her now?" Mammy stared at me, expressionless. For a minute I thought she'd finally lost the last functions of speech, but she opened her mouth and pulled the words from deep in her throat.

"Maisy wanted to go," she said simply.

I didn't waste time feeling sorry for myself over her abandonment; she'd stayed with me longer than she'd been bound, long after I'd stopped truly needing her. Fighting the urge to go had probably even made her sick.

"Will she be happy?" I whispered, thinking of our lives together since we'd left the mountain. Maisy had never been completely comfortable away from the mountain, a mildly unpleasant discomposure that we'd shared. But we'd made the best of it by necessity; it hadn't been safe to return until we'd been called back.

Mammy didn't bother to answer. She didn't have to. I knew.

On the way down the mountain, trying to keep my eyes from the rearview mirror, I thought of the congregation in the woods, names and faces I couldn't recall, passed out of

152

this place and taken over to another by an old woman barely clinging to this life herself. Mammy and I would join them in time. I allowed myself one glance in the mirror, finding the flames in the dark that matched my own.